1 MONTH OF
FREE
READING

at
www.ForgottenBooks.com

By purchasing this book you are eligible for one month membership to ForgottenBooks.com, giving you unlimited access to our entire collection of over 1,000,000 titles via our web site and mobile apps.

To claim your free month visit:
www.forgottenbooks.com/free919669

ISBN 978-0-265-98801-5
PIBN 10919669

This book is a reproduction of an important historical work. Forgotten Books uses
state-of-the-art technology to digitally reconstruct the work, preserving the original format
whilst repairing imperfections present in the aged copy. In rare cases, an imperfection in
the original, such as a blemish or missing page, may be replicated in our edition. We do,
however, repair the vast majority of imperfections successfully; any imperfections that
remain are intentionally left to preserve the state of such historical works.

Portrait of a Lady . . .

then and now!

Thrilling similarity of the mode
. . . the 1897 hip - length
basque that made grandma
such a charming lady, in a
new 1937 version that will
make you charming too. Stun-
ning two piece olive green
sheer wool costume with
black satin blouse and black
persian cloth trim, $29.75.
Black felt hat with persian
trim, $5.00. Matrix shoes,
black suede with clever
stitching, $8.75. Black suede
bag, $3.98. Gloves $2.98.

ZCMI
America's First Department Store

87 Years of Transportation Progress

The Mormon Trail still was dusty with wagon trains when the Aurora Branch Railroad, forerunner of the Burlington, commenced operations over strap-iron rails on September 2, 1850.

A dozen years after the exodus from Nauvoo, Burlington rails were following the fresh ruts of Mormon wagon trains westward across Iowa.

The Spring of 1882 saw the Burlington in Denver—a new transportation artery dedicated to the development of the Rocky Mountain West.

By the Fall of 1897, when the Improvement Era was founded by Heber J. Grant, the Burlington had become a transportation system operating more than 7,000 miles of railroad. We thought we had come a long way.

But, as the last 40 years have eloquently proved, the growth of the West and the Burlington had just begun. Population, industry and agriculture have doubled, trebled, quadrupled. The Burlington Lines have expanded to 12,000 miles, reaching 14 states. Freight and passenger trains operate at speeds undreamed of a few short years ago. Travelers aboard luxurious streamline Zephyrs now traverse in fleeting hours distances that took intrepid emigrants weary weeks.

Again we say that we have come a long way, much of it together, and the Burlington takes this occasion of the 40th anniversary of the Improvement Era to salute its friends and patrons in the Rocky Mountain West, and to predict that 40 years hence we can repeat: "We have come a long way."

WHAT LEADERS ARE SAYING

Burley, Idaho.
September 18, 1937.
"Every number of the *Era*, beginning with volume one, has come to our home. Were my wishes granted, the *Era* would be found in every Latter-day Saint home in our stake. There could not be greater spiritual help. My bound volumes are invaluable as reference books.
"Sincerely,
(Signed)   *David R. Langlois,"
President of Burley Stake.*

Overton, Nevada,
September 17, 1937
"As a missionary from November, 1899, to March, 1902, the *Era* came as one visiting from home. It has been a member of our family since 1904. We have enjoyed its pages, and appreciate its influence. Our aim in the Moapa Stake is to have an *Era* in every home.
"Respectfully,
(Signed)   *Willard L. Jones,"
President of Moapa Stake.*

September 25, 1937.
"The success of the Long Beach Stake in placing *The Improvement Era* in the homes of Latter-day Saints is due principally to the firm conviction we have that *The Improvement Era* is the greatest missionary force in the Church today.
"Many of our families would no more think of refusing to subscribe for the *Era* than they would to turn down an official call for missionary service. We know that homes where the *Era* is received and read enjoy rich spiritual blessings which would not come to them otherwise.
"Our Stake *Era* Director is a man whose life's profession is salesmanship and he has accepted the appointment of *Era* Director as a call to missionary service. The Lord is blessing him with the ability to instill into the hearts of his co-workers the spirit of missionary service of the *Era*. Recently upon his recommendation the new group of Stake Missionaries adopted the placement of *Eras* as their special missionary project during the winter. We are looking for some pleasant surprises from this source.
"With sincere appreciation for the outstanding magazine you are giving us,
"Sincerely your brother,
(Signed)   *J. W. Jones,"
President of Long Beach Stake.*

July 22, 1937.
". . . I know of no magazine of equal standard and the quality of the material is unsurpassed. I congratulate you and wish you continued success.
"Your brother in the Gospel,
(Signed)   *George Albert Smith,"
Of the Council of the Twelve.*

(Continued on page 660)

The "ERA'S" *First Savings Bank Advertiser*

First Zion's Savings Bank ad in Volume I, Number 1, of the Era, 40 Years Ago

SAVE YOUR MONEY AND WHEN YOU GET A DOLLAR

DEPOSIT IT WITH

DIRECTORS:
Wilford Woodruff, President,
George Q. Cannon, Vice-President,
George M. Cannon, Cashier,
Joseph F. Smith,
Lorenzo Snow,
Francis M. Lyman,
Heber J. Grant,
Angus M. Cannon,
T. G. Webber,
James Jack,
E. R. Clawson,
George Reynolds,
L. John Nuttall.

ZION'S SAVINGS BANK AND TRUST COMPANY,
1, 3, & 5 MAIN ST., SALT LAKE CITY, UTAH.

Forty years ago, the same year in which the Brigham Young Monument was unveiled on Zion's Savings Bank corner, this bank extended the hand of fellowship to the infant magazine, **The Improvement Era.** "Zion's" believed in the need for such a magazine and in the ability of its business and editorial staffs, which included Heber J. Grant and Thomas Hull, business managers, and Joseph F. Smith and B. H. Roberts, editors.

In the very first issue, Zion's Savings Bank & Trust Company became the magazine's first savings bank advertiser. A copy of this ad is reproduced above. The message of that ad, and the bank's same message to "Era" readers after 40 years, is,

Save your money and deposit it with

ZION'S SAVINGS BANK & TRUST CO.

MAIN AT SOUTH TEMPLE—SALT LAKE CITY

OFFICERS

HEBER J. GRANT	PRESIDENT
JOHN F. BENNETT	VICE-PRESIDENT
GEORGE S. SPENCER	VICE-PRESIDENT
WILLARD R. SMITH	CASHIER
WILLIAM McEWAN	ASST. CASHIER & TRUST OFFICER
J. FORBES DONE	ASST. CASHIER
WM. T. PATRICK	ASST. CASHIER
CLARON O. SPENCER	ASST. TRUST OFFICER

DIRECTORS

HEBER J. GRANT	ARTHUR WINTER	GEORGE S. SPENCER	J. REUBEN CLARK, JR.
ASAHEL H. WOODRUFF	WILLARD T. CANNON	WALDEMAR VAN COTT	DAVID O. McKAY
LEWIS TELLE CANNON	JOSEPH FIELDING SMITH	GEORGE J. CANNON	HERBERT A. SNOW
JOHN F. BENNETT	WILLARD R. SMITH	ORVAL W. ADAMS	

The Improvement Era

"The Glory of God is Intelligence"

NOVEMBER, 1937
VOLUME 40   NUMBER 11

"THE VOICE OF THE CHURCH"

OFFICIAL ORGAN OF THE PRIESTHOOD QUORUMS, MUTUAL IMPROVEMENT ASSOCIATIONS, DEPARTMENT OF EDUCATION, MUSIC COMMITTEE, WARD TEACHERS, AND OTHER AGENCIES OF THE CHURCH OF JESUS CHRIST OF LATTER-DAY SAINTS.

Heber J. Grant,
John A. Widtsoe,
      Editors
Richard L. Evans,
      Managing Editor
Marba C. Josephson,
      Associate Editor
George Q. Morris, *General Mgr.*
Clarissa A. Beesley, *Associate Mgr.*
J. K. Orton, *Business Mgr.*

TABLE OF CONTENTS

The Cover
OUR Fortieth Anniversary cover was drawn by *The Improvement Era's* staff artist, Fielding K. Smith. It uses the architecture of the Latter-day Saint Temples as the symbol of forty years of change and progress. The lower figure is the profile of the Manti, Utah, Temple, with its Nineteenth Century architecture. The spires of the Salt Lake Temple break through the center, and the top figure is an exaggerated conception of the L. D. S. Alberta Temple (Cardston, Canada) showing what may well be the temple of the future. The horse and buggy below and the airplane above show through what era our people have seen the world progress, in their travel to and from the Temples of the Living God.

WHAT LEADERS ARE SAYING
(Continued from page 658)

July 23, 1937.
". . . I sincerely congratulate you together with your associates on the way in which you are directing the affairs of the *Era*.

"May the future be full of joy and success for you and your co-workers.
"Sincerely your brother,
(Signed)   *Reed Smoot.*"
    Of the Council of the Twelve.

London, W. C. 1.
July 9, 1936.
". . . I congratulate you most heartily upon the growing popularity of the *Era*.
"With cordial good wishes.
"Sincerely your brother,
(Signed)   *Joseph F. Merrill.*"
    Of the Council of the Twelve.

5 Gordon Square,
London, W. C. 1.
August 31, 1937.
"The *Era* is glorious. We enjoy it immensely.
"Very sincerely yours,
(Signed)   *Amy Brown Lyman.*"
    Directing Women Activities in Europe.

Minneapolis, Minnesota,
September, 1937.
"It has been my good fortune to receive every number of the *Era* published. The North Central States Mission considers the *Era* 'The Voice of the Church,' the second best literature agency for stimulating life in the mission, and for converting souls, the Book of Mormon alone excepted.
"Sincerely yours,
(Signed)   *D. A. Broadbent.*"
    President of the North Central States Mission.
(Continued on page 695)

EXECUTIVE AND EDITORIAL OFFICES:
50 North Main Street, Salt Lake City, Utah

Copyright 1937, by the Young Men's Mutual Improvement Association Corporation of the Church of Jesus Christ of Latter-day Saints. All rights reserved. Subscription price, $2.00 a year, in advance; 20c Single Copy.

Entered at the Post Office, Salt Lake City, Utah, as second-class matter. Acceptance for mailing at special rate of postage provided for in section 1103, Act of October, 1917, authorized July 2, 1918.

The Improvement Era is not responsible for unsolicited manuscripts, but welcomes contributions. All manuscripts must be accompanied by sufficient postage for delivery and return.

A MAGAZINE FOR EVERY MEMBER OF THE FAMILY

Gasoline and Oil
have changed, too!

Today....

your sleek streamlined automobile with its high-compression, smooth-running engine, could not have been developed without the advances that have been made in refining gasoline and motor oil. In the intermountain territory, Pep 88 and Vico set the pace for modern performance. These products are made in one of America's most modern refineries where the latest developments of science are utilized to produce gasoline and oil that give you enjoyable and economical motoring.

UTAH OIL REFINING COMPANY

STATIONS EVERYWHERE IN UTAH AND IDAHO

Deseret News Photo.

PRESIDENT HEBER J GRANT

WORLD *head of the Church of Jesus Christ of Latter-day Saints and
beloved leader of his people as he appears seated at his desk in the
Church Office building, Salt Lake City, as he approaches the Eighty-first
Anniversary of his birth which occurs November 22, 1937.*

Mural in the Union Pacific Depot, Salt
Lake City, showing the driving of the
golden spike at Promontory, Utah, in
1869, which marked the beginning of
transcontinental railroad service in the
United States.

ON behalf of the Union Pacific Railroad and its
employees, I am happy to extend greetings and
best wishes to President Heber J. Grant and the
great Mormon people and to heartily congratulate The Jmprovement Era on its Fortieth
Anniversary.

Wm Jeffers

President

UNION PACIFIC RAILROAD
OMAHA, NEBRASKA

Mural in the Union Pacific Depot in
Salt Lake City depicting the con-
quest of the Inland West by Brigham
Young and the Mormon people.

A Call to Church Leaders:

"No man can proclaim this Gospel by the Spirit of the Living God unless that man is living his religion."

BY

PRESIDENT HEBER J. GRANT

I AM very pleased indeed to express my deep appreciation of our Conference, from start to finish.

I am grateful for the Gospel of Jesus Christ. I am thankful for the devotion of the Latter-day Saints as a whole.

I announced here at the Priesthood meeting last night and I decided to announce it again that we expect all the General Officers of the Church, each and every one of them, from this very day, to be absolute, full-tithepayers, to really and truly observe the Word of Wisdom; and we ask all of the officers of the Church and all members of the General Boards, and all Stake and Ward officers, if they are not living the Gospel and honestly and conscientiously paying their tithing, to kindly step aside, unless from this day they live up to these provisions.

We have undertaken a most stupendous work and there will be no difficulty whatever in carrying out that great work. We will have an abundance to take care of every living Latter-day Saint who is in distress. Mind you, when I say Latter-day Saint I mean Latter-day Saint. I am not talking about idlers. I am not talking about people that want to lie down and let somebody else take care of them—I am talking of Latter-day Saints. If the people will pay their tithing and if they will keep the Word of Wisdom, and will actually, really, and for a fact, fast two meals once a month and give the equivalent, we will be able to carry forward our Security Plan without any trouble whatever.

It is simply marvelous that people can live on eleven cents, some of them—two meals a day once each month for twelve months in the year—twenty-four meals on a half a cent a meal. [Or at least, so their fast offerings would indicate.]

We feel that in all the stakes of Zion, every stake president, every counselor to a stake president, every stake clerk, and every high councillor, standing at the head of the people in the stake—we ask them to kindly step aside unless they are living up to these laws. They are given the responsibility of presiding, and every officer who is a presiding officer should say from today: "I am going to serve the Lord, so that my example will be worthy of imitation."

No man can teach the Word of Wisdom, by the Spirit of God, who does not live it. No man can proclaim this Gospel by the Spirit of the Living God unless that man is living his religion; and with this great undertaking that we have before us now

Out of the 108th Semi-annual Conference, held in the Tabernacle in Salt Lake City, October 1st to 3rd inclusive, there came from the leaders of the Church such messages, spoken with power and authority, and pertaining so vitally to our temporal and spiritual well-being, that all of them should be in the hands of every member of the Church, to be read and re-read. Doubtless the most significant message of the Conference was the one reprinted here which President Grant left sounding in the hearts of the Latter-day Saints there assembled as he closed the final session.

we must renew our loyalty to God, and I believe beyond a shadow of doubt that God inspires and blesses, and multiplies our substance when we are honest with Him. We do not want in this day a repetition of what the scriptures tell us was the condition in years gone by, wherein the Lord declares that He had been robbed, because of the failure of the people to live the financial law that God has revealed.

Now, I pray from the bottom of my heart that God will give each and every man and woman who holds an office in any stake or ward the spirit and the feeling and the determination from this day, to renew his covenants with God, to live his religion; and if we are too weak to do these things, we should step aside and let somebody else take our place.

The Word of Wisdom, we are told, is such that it can be kept by "the weak and the weakest of all Saints." I have heard that some of the members of Boards, after the law was passed legalizing beer, said: "Well, I do declare, now I am entitled to have a glass of beer." No Latter-day Saint is entitled to anything that is contrary to the mind and will of the Lord, and the Word of Wisdom is the mind and the will of the Lord.

I want you to know that this will make no difference to me personally, but as the shepherd of the flock, the day has come, in my judgment and in the judgment of my associates, that we must live up to and be loyal to this work and serve God with all our heart, might, mind, and strength, if we are to accomplish what the Lord wants us to do.

I thank you all for your presence here. I thank the Lord for the splendid Conference we have had. In so far as God has given me the power to do so, I pray God to bless you one and all. I pray God to bless all the Latter-day Saints. I pray God to bless every soul that has good intentions, and to strengthen him and her in their determination to keep the commandments of the Lord. I love the Lord; I love the Latter-day Saints; I love the honest world over; I have no animosity against any living soul. The Gospel of Jesus Christ is one of forgiveness of wrong-doing. It is a part of the Gospel to forgive those who have done wrong, when they repent, but "By this ye may know if a man repenteth of his sins—behold, he will confess them and forsake them." He will do them no more.

The time has expired.

May God's blessing be with each and all of you, and with all the Saints, and with all the honest the world over, I pray in the name of Jesus Christ, our Redeemer. Amen.

(These were the President's closing words at the 108th Semi-annual Conference in the Tabernacle, Salt Lake City, Sunday afternoon, October 3, 1937.)

The CHURCH LOOKS

●

By J. REUBEN CLARK, JR.

Of the First Presidency

I.

THE days of our infancy and early childhood are filled with a growing awareness of time, space, gravity, the elements, and bodily well-being; and thence to the grave is a constant struggle to overcome the handicaps—the inhibitions and limitations—imposed by these physical incidents of our being. To the gaining of the experiences of mastering these incidents must be added the experiences having to do with making the biological part of man articulate and with the cultivation and interchange of thought. The nearer comes the conquest of these, the nearer come men together, and the nearer men approach one another, the nearer comes the universal brotherhood of men and their ultimate perfection.

But whatever may be the conquests of man, these limitations and inhibitions remain to clog his advance and intercourse with others. Time, space, gravity, the elements, disease are constantly with him; they assert themselves with disaster the instant he ignores or forgets them. All that man may ever do is to escape or thwart their operation by the use of other laws. In so far as man succeeds, he performs miracles.

During the ages, man has gone long distances towards his ultimate conquest of all these. From the shelter of a tree or cave, through the lean-to, the log hut, the adobe house, to the giant structure of steel, concrete, and glass, housing a city within its four walls; from the lone footpath in the forest, through the dirt road, the dust and mud of the city street, the paved sidewalk, the paved thoroughfares, to the great concrete ribbon spanning a continent; from the pack of a few pounds on a man's back, through the oxcart, the horse and buggy, to the railroad with its thousands of tons, and the auto truck; from the fleetest runner, through the pony express, the fast mail train, to the airplane traveling a fourth as fast as the earth revolves on its axis; from the shout that, with fair air, carried a few hundred feet, through the telephone linking cities, to the radio carrying the voice round the globe with the speed of light (we

have yet to reach the speed of thought); from the passing down of story and song by word of mouth, through the invention of written characters, the writing by hand on bulky scrolls of parchment, on rushes, on paper, then to the printing press with its plain black letters, through woodcuts, steel engravings, lithographs, photogravures, to gorgeous pages in natural colors; from the mangled, gangrenous broken leg demanding a life, through amputation with hideous pain without anesthetic, to the most refined and delicate painless operation upon the very seat of the mind itself,—all these but indicate man's conquests of his inhibitions and limitations.

Yet time, space, gravity, the elements, disease, still inexorably rule the world; and death waits patiently, silently, at the end of the path of life. So shallow is man's success that a faulty iron girder, a weak rail joint, a loose connection, a poorly tempered wire brace, a blundering blade, and his conquest is swallowed up without a ripple in the ocean of law and force that rules the universe. Surely man should make his boasts under his breath.

But however stable or unstable, however complete or incomplete these conquests may be, they mark human progress—how great relatively we may not measure for we do not know the ultimate, yet man seems to have come great distances. But these conquests of energy and force make human progress, add to human comfort and well-being, increase knowledge and quicken intelligence, and, above all (and this is the end of it all) promote human happiness, for the ancient prophet declared "Men are that they might have joy." Happiness comes in proportion as we lift ourselves beyond the reach of the penalty of earth law; and perfection comes nearer with happiness.

Thus all knowledge in whatever field it may rest, all uplifting human experience, all the ennobling activities of men, all truths of the universe, aid men to rise above and save them from the inhibitions and limitations of the flesh. The Psalmist of old sang "The law is the truth." and Jesus said, "Ye shall

INTO THE FUTURE

THE CHURCH, ABSORBING THE TRUTH OF THE PAST, WILL MAKE ITS OWN THE TRUTH OF THE FUTURE TO THE ULTIMATE PERFECTION OF ITS MEMBERS.

A ND THE FORWARD LOOK FINDS THESE THINGS TO BE TRUE EVEN AS THEY HAVE BEEN IN THE PAST—

T HAT WHILE MAN'S CONQUESTS OF FORCE AND ENERGY ARE YET SHALLOW AND UN- STABLE, THEY LEAD HIM UPWARDS TOWARDS PERFECTION.

T HAT ALL TRUTH IS INTEGRALLY PART OF THE GOSPEL OF JESUS CHRIST AND LEADS US TOWARDS PERFECTION.

T HAT MATERIAL REWARDS MAY COME WITH- OUT EFFORT OR DESERVINGNESS—BUT NOT SO WITH THINGS OF THE SPIRIT.

T HAT INDIVIDUALISM IN SPIRITUALITY IS FUNDAMENTAL.

T HAT THE PHYSICAL INHIBITIONS AND LIMI- TATIONS OF THE FLESH, AND ALSO THOSE ENCUMBERING THE SPIRIT BECAUSE OF MOR- TALITY, MUST BE CONQUERED BEFORE PERFEC- TION CAN COME.

T HAT "THIS GOSPEL OF THE KINGDOM SHALL BE PREACHED IN ALL THE WORLD"—AND THAT "EVERY KNEE SHALL BOW AND EVERY TONGUE CONFESS THAT JESUS IS THE CHRIST," —THE CHURCH IS WORLD-WIDE.

know the truth, and the truth shall make you free."

A S we make these truths our own, so perfection approaches. It was by His perfect knowledge of truth —and He said to Thomas, "I am the way, the truth, and the life"— that Jesus turned water into wine. multiplied the loaves and fishes, es- caped from the threatening mob on the edge of the cliff at Nazareth and again within the temple walls at Je- rusalem, that took Him into the room with closed windows and doors to visit the fearsome, questioning, doubting Apostles; indeed, that brought Him forth from the tomb the First Fruits of the Resurrection. He had said to the angered mob in His great sermon on the Good Shep- herd:

Therefore doth my Father love me, be- cause I lay down my life, that I might take it again. No man taketh it from me, but I lay it down of myself. I have power to lay it down, and I have power to take it again. This commandment have

I received from my Father. *(John* 10:17-18)

Hannah prayed of old: "The Lord is a God of knowledge."

II.

So the Church and its members must seek for and cherish knowl- edge; the finding and learning of truth must always take their first thought, because knowledge of truth leads toward perfection, and the Master said, "Be ye perfect even as your Father in Heaven is per- fect."

Since knowledge of truth leads to perfection, and since the Gospel is God's plan to bring men to per- fection, our affirmation that all truth is part of the Gospel becomes clear, and to those who have not followed the reasons, the declaration of our Articles of Faith assumes now an added meaning when we say:

Indeed we may say that we follow the

ILLUSTRATED BY
FIELDING K. SMITH

admonition of Paul—We believe all things, we hope all things, we have endured many things, and hope to be able to endure all things. If there is anything virtuous, lovely or of good report or praiseworthy, we seek after these things.

Thus the Church glories in all progress and advancement in science, in art, in literature, and in every avenue of human endeavor and activity, for every conquest of a physical inhibition or limitation upon the freedom of the human soul makes for perfection. The Church makes its own every truth that comes. It casts away all error. It suspends adoption where truth and error still contend, until truth prevails and bares her face, then it takes her to its bosom and makes her part of itself. The Church takes all things of material progress and uses them for the convenience, comfort, and advancement of the members, for their edification, education, and culture, for their social and economic welfare and security; no truth, no principle of well-being or right living is discountenanced, withheld, or forbidden. This has been the rule of the Church from the beginning.

III.

BUT the things already spoken of only lead out toward perfection but not to it, for perfection may not be reached by mastery over the material things alone.

Perfection means also the subjugation of the intellectual and spiritual limitations and inhibitions which are incident to the flesh.

But there is an essential and fundamental difference between conquest and achievement in the physical and in the spiritual world. One need not do the works of Morse or Edison or Marconi in order fully to enjoy and use the telegraph, the telephone, the gramophone, or the radio; nor need one do the works of the Wrights in order to enjoy and use to the full the airplane. The most ignorant and depraved of men may use all these things for his own purposes, to serve his own ends, good or bad, for the benefit or injury of others, as fully as they who made them. The user has merely to pay the money price and then have all of the power, all the effective use which he who created them had or can have.

So likewise it is with the works of the great artists, sculptors, musicians, dramatists, and men of letters. Save only the creative joy which those alone who make may know, these masterpieces may be

668

fully understood, appreciated, and enjoyed by any one without doing the works of the creator.

But it is not so with the things of the spirit. One must do the works of Elijah if one would know his joy, have part in his blessings, share his glory, exercise his power and authority, and do the things he did. And surely the power to bring rain to a famine-stricken land, to call down fire from heaven, to cause the starving widow's barrel of meal not to waste, her cruse of oil not to fail, to restore to life her dead son, to declare the past and foretell the future—surely these things are beyond compare; they may not be valued, nor purchased, nor hired; they are beyond price. Here the

works and the use are companions that never part. Do Elijah's works if you would use and enjoy his powers.

So it comes that in affairs of the spirit, the doing of the works and the use of the resulting spiritual power, are not only inseparable but wholly individual. They are not to be bought as Elisha taught Naaman and as Simon the Sorcerer learned from the rebuke of Peter: "Thy money perish with thee because thou hast thought that the gift of God may be purchased with money." Save for the atoning sacrifice of the Son and the doing of certain initiatory rites for the dead (and even these must be accepted and adopted by the dead), nothing can be vicariously done, in matters of the spirit, by one for another. Everyone must do his own work, if he would have the power and authority.

IV.

Individualism in spirituality is fundamental to Christianity. Thus Jesus, taking leave of His Apostles and about to ascend into heaven, said unto them: "Go ye into all the world and preach the Gospel to every creature; he that believeth and is baptized shall be saved, and he that believeth not shall be

damned." Jesus had earlier said to Nicodemus: "Except a man be born of water and of the Spirit, he cannot enter into the kingdom of God."

The Lord has many times repeated these same injunctions and principles to the Latter-day Church. There can be no question but that every ear must hear and be given the choice of living or refusing the Gospel.

To leave no doubt in the minds of the Apostles who were with Him in Palestine that He meant every creature in the whole world, and not merely among those who were called His chosen people — Jesus declared to them in the great discourse on the Mount of Olives :

And this Gospel of the Kingdom shall be preached in all the world, for a witness unto all nations: and then shall the end come. (*Matt.* 24:14.)

In this day the Lord has declared the Gospel should be preached "at all times and in all places," "among all nations," in "all the world,"— "and for this cause, that men might be partakers of the glories which were to be revealed." Again He declared, speaking to the Prophet in relation to Sidney Rigdon and Frederick G. Williams:

That thereby they may be perfected in their ministry for the salvation of Zion, and of the nations of Israel, and of the Gentiles, as many as will believe.

That through your administration they may receive the word, and through their administration the word may go forth unto the ends of the earth, unto the Gentiles first, and then, behold, and lo, they shall turn unto the Jews.

And then cometh the day when the arm of the Lord shall be revealed in power in convincing the nations, the heathen nations, the house of Joseph, of the Gospel of their salvation.

For it shall come to pass in that day, that every man shall hear the fulness of the Gospel in his own tongue, and in his own language, through those who are ordained unto this power, by the administration of the Comforter, shed forth upon them for the revelation of Jesus Christ. (*Doc and Cov.* 90:8-11.)

The Lord reiterated these fundamentals time and again: the Gospel is to be preached "unto Gentile and unto Jew;" "the poor and the meek shall hear the Gospel," and "those who sit in darkness and in the region and shadow of death."

The part of the Church in all this is clear and explicit:

For verily, the sound must go forth from this place into all the world, and unto the uttermost parts of the earth. (*Doc. and Cov.*, 58:64.)

And again:

Hearken, and lo, a voice as of one sent down from on high, who is mighty and powerful, whose going forth is unto the ends of the earth, yea, whose voice is unto men—Prepare ye the way of the Lord, make His paths straight.

The keys of the kingdom of God are committed unto man on the earth, and from thence shall the Gospel roll forth unto the ends of the earth, as the stone which is cut out of the mountain without hands shall roll forth, until it has filled the whole earth.

V.

So the Lord has spoken. From His words, these things clearly appear:

Every man, woman, and child, in every country, Christian, Hebrew, heathen, must hear the Gospel in its fullness—the rich, the poor, the meek, the haughty. The Lord has expressly told us: "I am no respecter of persons."

Thus every person shall make his own mind what his life shall be. None shall make it for him. Whether he will be satisfied with that part of salvation which pertains to the physical world, or whether he shall go on and add to this the salvation and exaltation of the spiritual universe, is for his own choice. And perhaps there should be here recalled the Lord's saying that in reality "All spirit is matter, but it is more fine or pure, and can only be discerned by purer eyes, we cannot see it, but when our bodies are purified we shall see that it is all matter."

For him who would throw off also the inhibitions and limitations of the flesh in matters affecting the spirit, for him indeed who would conquer the flesh for the blessings of the spirit, there is a joy awaiting which exceeds all power of description,—because words are made to describe the physical world, they are wanting to express even the highest pleasures and feelings of mortality; when the lofty emotions of the spirit are conceived, we must content ourselves with the flashing, tear-wet eye, the ennobled countenance, the sobbing of joy, an exaltation of mind and spirit which no pen can write or tongue tell.

These two conquests—the throwing off of the physical limitations and inhibitions that control and hold down our physical activities and the rising above the limitations and inhibitions of the flesh in matters of the spirit—are each within the ultimate reach of everyone of God's children who is willing to live the Gospel and make the needed struggle and sacrifice. Neither conquest can be fully made in the flesh, but the beginnings made in mortality can be completed in immortality. This is man's destiny. And the Gospel plan through which he reaches this end, is so plain and simple that "a wayfaring man, though a fool, need not err therein."

VI.

The Church is the organization which God has set up to help men in their struggles against the limitations and inhibitions of the flesh as affecting the spirit and its manifestations and development. It is as nearly perfect as mortals permit it to be; greater perfection will come just as soon as men can understand and use it. The Lord has never revealed His mind and will beyond man's power of comprehension, and when man has shown his confirmed unwillingness to follow the plan and live the law revealed,

the Lord has taken each away and given a less perfect plan and lower law, as He did to Israel under Moses.

In all times, the Lord's plan—His Church—has provided for the physical well-being of the people. The divine plan calls for the perfect body as well as the perfected spirit. There is an intimate and not understood—if indeed it be at all comprehensible by the human mind—relationship between biological man and spiritual man. Bodily well-being,—the feeding of the hungry, the giving of health to the diseased body, the curing of the maimed, the halt, the blind, the deaf, the dumb, the thrusting out of death itself and re-enthroning life in the mortal body —was a large part of Christ's work on earth. He would not have done this if, under His plan, the body were to be ignored, or mistreated, or debauched. The Church of Christ, to carry out His purposes, must have this twin purpose: The protection and perfecting of the body, the perfecting of the Spirit. To bring this about in every individual is the purpose of the Church.

Now the Lord has said that His plan is that every creature on the earth, that every nation, that every people,—each and every one must "hear the fullness of the Gospel in his own tongue and in his own language." So to carry this Gospel is the mission and the destiny of the Church. The responsibility for initiating the plan, for setting up the Church, and for presently directing it has been given to us of America. But it is not our Church: it belongs to all God's children and as much to one as to another. For those to whom God has entrusted the preaching of this Gospel and the spreading of it through the earth, there are no greater blessings awaiting than await anyone who holds the Priesthood and lives the Gospel, whoever he may be and wherever he lives; but upon us there rests an all but crushing responsibility that, not fully met, will bring to us not only loss of blessing but great condemnation as well.

So it is the mission of the Church to see that "the Gospel rolls forth unto the ends of the earth, as the stone which is cut out of the mountain without hands shall roll forth, until it has filled the whole earth."

Where the Gospel goes, there must go the Church also, until it fills the earth.

So not America only, nor America and Europe, but the whole earth is the Lord's and all that in it are. And His Church filling the earth will bring to its peoples and to all of them the peace, the joy, and the fullness and richness of life which the power of the evil and the base now denies to them. Ultimately "every knee shall bow and every tongue confess that Jesus is the Christ."

SOME FACTS ABOUT THE CHURCH FORTY YEARS AGO—AND NOW		
1897		1936
252,000	(approximately) Number of Members	760,690
37	Number of Stakes	118
466	Number of Wards	1,001
17	Number of Missions	35
4	Number of Temples	7
1496	Number of full-time Missionaries	1940

PRESIDENT GRANT'S
• FIRST "ERA" ARTICLE

EDITOR'S NOTE:—We here reprint the first signed article by President Heber J. Grant to appear in "The Improvement Era." It is found on pages 395 to 398 of Volume I—nearly forty years ago, and is entitled "Recollections Awakened by the Late Semi-Centennial Celebration."

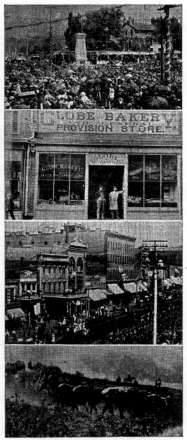

OLD SALT LAKE CITY SCENES. TOP: DEDICATION OF BRIGHAM YOUNG MONUMENT, SOUTH TEMPLE AND MAIN STREET, 1897; SECOND: THE OLD GLOBE BAKERY; THIRD: A PARADE OF THE RETURNING SPANISH-AMERICAN WAR VETERANS; BOTTOM: SCENES OF 1847 REENACTED IN 1897.

D URING the recent celebration of the Semi-Centennial Anniversary of the entrance of the Pioneers into Salt Lake Valley, very many thoughts crowded themselves upon my mind, as I contrasted the difference between the Salt Lake Valley of that day and the Salt Lake Valley of today.

I was seated in one of the large show windows of the main store building of Zion's Cooperative Mercantile Institution, as the Semi-Centennial procession moved down Main Street, and I contrasted that immense structure in which I was seated, with the one and two-story adobe dwellinghouse which at one time stood upon that identical spot, and in which residence I first saw the light of day. The house was built by my father, who died when I was a babe of nine days, and I lived there until I was a little over six years old, when I moved with my mother to Second East Street, where I now reside.

Having virtually seen Main Street change from a village thoroughfare to a business avenue, I recalled the time when Zion's Savings Bank, a splendid building of five stories, was occupied by the home of the late Daniel H. Wells, and in my mind's eye I saw the high rock wall which separated the home of my childhood from that of "Squire Wells." Everybody familiarly called him "Squire Wells" in those days. Two more lovable or kinder men never lived than my childhood neighbors, President Daniel H. Wells on the north, and Bishop Edward Hunter on the south. Another kind friend was Joseph B. Elder, who recently died in the Fourteenth Ward. He had a little frame grocery store and cooper shop which occupied the corner where now stands the Godbe-Pitt drug store. Many and many an hour have I spent as a child sitting in his store and chatting with him.

As I thought of the fine structure known as the "Hooper & Eldredge Block," I recalled the familiar home of the late Bishop Edward Hunter, which originally stood upon that ground, and scores of incidents and sayings of his which were amusing, interesting, and instructive came to my mind, prominent among them being his oft-repeated counsel, "Pay your tithing, brethren, and be blessed." Above all I recall his wonderful kindness to me in childhood days. I thought of the hundreds of times that I had crept through the pole fence which divided his home from ours, to play with his boys, and I also remember climbing very often the board fence south of his barn, to romp and play with one of the most beloved companions of my childhood, George Hooper, son of the late Captain William H. Hooper, who was called to his eternal rest in his youth. Where George's home then stood, now stands the substantial "Hooper Block."

As I looked across the street at the "Constitution Building," I remembered the time when the "Old Constitution Building" stood there, and as I gazed at the "Home Fire Building," I remembered the old "Globe Bakery," and barber shop adjoining, which occupied the site when I was but five or six years old.

In looking up the street at the Pioneer Monument in stone and bronze, I recalled many, many incidents in the life of Brigham Young, and one of them of my childhood days I will relate, as it illustrates what it is impossible to do in stone and bronze, viz: the love which filled Brigham Young's heart for his fellowmen.

WHEN I was about six years old, in the winter of 1862, the sleighing was very good and as I had no opportunity of cutter-riding in those days, none of our family possessing a sleigh or team, boy-like, I used quite frequently to run into the street, and "hang on behind" some of the outfits which passed our home, and after riding a block or two would jump off and run back.

On one of these occasions I got on the sleigh belonging to President Brigham Young, and as all who were acquainted with him know, he was very fond of a fine team, and was given to driving quite rapidly. I therefore found myself skimming along with such speed that I dared not jump off, and after riding some time I became very cold. President Young happening to notice me hanging on his sleigh immediately called out: "Brother Isaac, stop!" He then had his driver, Isaac Wilson, get out and pick me up and tuck me snugly under the robes on the front seat. President Young waited some time before saying anything to me, but finally he asked, "Are you warm?" and when I answered "Yes," he inquired my name and where I lived. He then talked to me in the most kindly manner, told me how much he had loved my father and what a good man he was, and expressed the hope that I would be as good as my father. Our conversation ended in his inviting me to come up to his office some day and have a chat with him. This I very soon afterwards did, and from the day of this childhood acquaintance with President Young, I ever found in calling at his office or home, a most hearty welcome, and I learned not only to respect and venerate him, but to love him with an affection akin to that which I imagined I would have felt for my own father had I been permitted to know and return a father's love.

In nothing did Brigham Young shine more than in his love for children, and they repaid his love with love and confidence in him. The people of the world, who knew him not, with their prejudices against his system of religion, no doubt think he was unworthy of respect, but those who, like myself, have known and loved him since childhood, can testify of his goodness and of his love for his fellows, and to be able to do this is of greater moment than to join in any degree of praise that may be accorded him on the score of his great achievements.

It would take too much space for me to relate all the feelings and memories that crowded upon each other while sitting in the Z. C. M. I. window looking upon the Semi-Centennial procession as it passed down East Temple Street, carrying with it the evidences of the peace, prosperity, progress, and happiness of the present day; nor can I write all I thought and felt as I contemplated the trials of the Pioneers as recollections of them were awakened by the passing of one of their "reproduced trains;" and the float of the "Sea Gulls," that brought up the remembrance of the mighty deliverance from starvation wrought out by these white-winged messengers of God destroying the crickets, which otherwise would have devoured the first crop of the Pioneers, and left them to perish of hunger in the wilderness.

This article is already long enough, but I can not close without saying that the grand celebration of Utah's Semi-Centennial was worthy of Utah's Pioneers; an honor to those who managed it; and on the other hand, the Utah Pioneers were worthy of just such a magnificent celebration.

HEBER J. GRANT.

OLD SALT LAKE CITY SCENES. TOP: AN OLD MULE CAR AND HORSE-DRAWN CARRIAGE AT SOUTH TEMPLE AND MAIN STREETS: SECOND: AN EARLY PICTURE OF Z. C. M. I.: THIRD: THE OLD CONSTITUTION BUILDING; FOURTH: LOOKING EAST ON FIRST SOUTH TOWARD THE SALT LAKE THEATRE; BOTTOM: BATHING AT BLACK ROCK IN 1880.

FORTY YEARS
of CHANGE

By GLYNN BENNION
Of the Church Historian's Office

SINCE THE "ERA" FIRST SAW THE LIGHT OF DAY THE WORLD HAS
SEEN MORE CHANGES THAN IN MANY CENTURIES BEFORE—
SOME IN THE NAME OF PROGRESS AND SOME IN THE NAME OF
LESS WORTHY THINGS. BUT MAN'S USE OF ALL IMPROVEMENTS
IS MORE IMPORTANT THAN THE MATERIAL THINGS OF WHICH
PROGRESS IS MADE.

I.

FROM our eminence of forty rungs up the ladder of time since *The Improvement Era* took the vacated place of the old *Contributor,* let us take a retrospective look at some of the things that have been happening in the meantime. It may help us to answer the questions: Where are we going?—and—How fast are we getting there?

In many respects the past forty years have been the most wonderful in the history of mankind. Surely the prophet Daniel glimpsed our time when he saw in the last days a people running to and fro under the stimulus of a great increase of knowledge. Greater scientific advances have been made during the past half century than during all the rest of recorded history. A catalogue of the new mechanical appliances of this period is breathtaking. So rapidly has this tremendous release of inventive energy propelled us into the machine age that the social and spiritual progress of the human family has apparently failed to keep pace with technological advance, and to some thinkers has come the fear that the new machinery will turn out to be a Frankenstein monster instead of a blessing. Let us examine, first, a few of the late outstanding inventions:

II.

BY 1897 the horseless carriage (the first one had been built by Elwood Haynes four years earlier) had captured the imagination of the public and was rapidly advancing toward the factory stage of production. Two years later at least three hundred of these gasoline-burning, horse-scaring contraptions

were upon the highways of the United States, snorting along at death-defying speeds of from eight to twelve miles an hour. Each year since that time has seen astonishing improvement in the economy of production, comfort, speed, and beauty of the automobile, until today the face of the land is covered with millions of them, scurrying, darting back and forth like a great swarm of frantic black beetles, crazily intent on their foolish errands.

In forty years the automobile industry has grown from scratch to the second largest business in the country, involving billions of dollars in wealth. Over twenty-eight million motor cars are now in use in the United States, and the wholesale value of new cars and accessories produced and sold last year was nearly four billion dollars. With this rapid growth has come a coincident expansion of the oil business and an era of road building. The continent is now banded with paved highways that reach from coast to coast, and the edges of

these are studded with service stations from whose nozzles this year will be poured eighteen billion gallons of gasoline—such a river of gasoline as will presently empty our great underground reservoirs of oil. In automobiling the native Yankee urge to get somewhere else fast has found a glorious release, and we have become a nation on wheels. Descendants of pioneer "wagon tramps" now follow the seasonal cycle of work and climate in trailers, and the perils and hazards seemingly requisite to mortal life which once were furnished by savages and wild animals are now furnished by the speed demon. A speeding motorist can now cover more miles in twenty minutes than his grandfather could make in a day; but blood stains and shattered glass mark the smooth, straight highways, and annually in the United States forty thousand lives are fed into this modern, streamlined Moloch.

MAIN STREET, SALT LAKE CITY, IN THE LATE
NINETEENTH CENTURY. (LOOKING NORTH FROM
SECOND SOUTH STREET.)

III.

IN 1897, a twenty-three year old Italian, named Guglielmo Marconi, who for several years had been intrigued by the theory that an electric current when started in a given direction follows a direct course without the assistance of a conductor, was busy perfecting an apparatus for wireless telegraphy. With a sensitive detector, capable of picking up ever so faint etheric vibrations, he was able in 1901 to receive wireless messages at Signal Hill, Newfoundland, originating at Poldhu station in England. So successful was he, in fact, that the Anglo-American Cable Company, fearing for their trade, compelled him to leave Newfoundland!

These achievements in wireless telegraphy greatly stimulated electrical engineers experimenting in the field of wireless telephony, and soon a new race of geniuses sprang up all over the country speaking of "audions" and "oscillions" and other words no layman can understand, but very evidently meaning what they said, for by 1915 they were able to transmit speech without the aid of wires from Arlington to Paris, a distance of 3,600 miles. In the wake of these achievements mushroom factories sprang up everywhere making radio receiving sets for individual use; a Federal commission had to be added to the already overstuffed bureaus of Washington to regulate conflicting sending stations, and now 25,000,000 sets throughout the United States may

A SCENE BEFORE EAGLE GATE, 1872.

make both day and night hideous with the shrieks of dying gun molls, the jittery beat of swing bands, and the fiendish wailing of anemic love songs which fatuous advertisers hope will increase the sales of coffee, cigarettes, and patent cure-alls. And yet this thing called radio, properly used, spreads tidings of truth over the face of the earth in the twinkling of an eye and brings men together in the common bond of the common heritage of the good things of earth.

IV.

MOTION PICTURES had a beginning in Thomas A. Edison's ingenious idea of capitalizing on a defect of the human eye called "persistence of vision." He noted that an impression on the retina lingers for a fiftieth part of a second after the scene exciting the impression has been removed. Accordingly, as early as 1879 he began experimenting with a lantern he called the "kinetoscope," an instrument by which many separate pictures per second were projected upon a screen, the interval during the change of pictures being so brief that to the eye it appeared one continuous presentation. The requirement of delicate precision in this machine, now called the cinematograph, was served by the Lumiere brothers of Paris, who in 1895 effected several improvements, and by 1911, with the addition of the multiple reel feature, the contrivance was ready to promote the vast new enterprise called the motion picture business. Technicolor and the synchronizing of voice

with picture are the most recent improvements added to motion pictures, this new form of the drama which has all but crowded the legitimate theatre off the earth, and which in the United States weekly attracts a throng equal to two-thirds of the entire population of the country. No device ever invented has more power for affecting the manners and thought of the public than the movies. There is reason, therefore, for anxiety regarding the morals and tastes of the public in the hands of mercenary czars whose chief study often is an analysis of the human weakness for being humbugged by cheap thrills.

V.

IN THE popular mind Edison is best remembered for the incandescent light, the phonograph, and the cinematograph, but the Patent Office shows that he was concerned with hundreds of other inventions, including the typewriter, the mimeograph, electric dynamo, railway signal system, motion picture camera, and photographic films, automobile starter, process for making plate glass, process for constructing concrete buildings, the electric lantern, and synthetic rubber. His discovery of most profound importance was perhaps that of the flow of electrons from hot filaments made during his early experiments with lamps, for from this observation has come the electronic tube, which in its myriad forms underlies radio broadcasting, long-distance telephoning, sound pictures, television, the electric eye, the X-ray, and a host of other devices. The United States Congress, in striking a medal for him in 1928, placed a value of nearly sixteen

billion dollars on his inventive contributions to humanity.

VI.

EVER since man first realized that he was condemned to crawl on the earth's crust for want of wings he has watched with envy the glorious flight of birds. And being really a supernatural creature, as proved by his rankling ambition to learn the secrets of immortality, to move beyond the bounds of his environment,

and to extend his dominion everywhere, he has from the beginning nursed the confidence that he would some day learn how to fly. The first thinkers of whom history gives account seriously proposed methods of aerial navigation. Archimedes, the Greek mathematician who lived several centuries before Christ, established the principles of mechanical flight which are now successfully applied. The Duke of Milan's dazzling jack-of-all-trades, Leon-

ardo da Vinci, made designs of a flap-wing affair, a helicopter, and a glider in the fifteenth century. But it was not until thirty-four years ago that a human being was carried from the ground in actual flight by mechanical means. On December 17, 1903, amid the Kill Devil sandhills of North Carolina, Wilbur and Orville Wright flew 852 feet in a kite-like apparatus which they had constructed after long study of all the accumulated theories of flight. This was the birth of the airplane.

Two years later these pioneer airmen made a non-stop flight of twenty-four miles, the airplane remaining aloft thirty-eight minutes. In 1909, the Frenchman, Bleriot, flew across the English Channel in twenty-three minutes. In 1911, Rogers crossed the United States in an airplane in forty-nine days. In 1919, Alcock and Brown made the first non-stop flight across the Atlantic. In 1924, the U. S. Army commenced the famous "Round the World" flight in May which was completed in August. During the same year Lieutenant Russell Maughan flew from New York to San Francisco in twenty-one hours. In 1927, Lindbergh flew from New York to Paris, 3,600 miles, in thirty-three hours. In 1933, Wiley Post flew around the world in seven days. In 1936, regular airmail service across the Pacific was inaugurated, and airlines within the United States carried 1,140,000 passengers.

No generation has been privileged to see so heroic a spectacle as we have seen enacted in the clouds by our pioneer pilots, most of whom fell to their deaths to advance the science of flying. What a horrible thought that all this inventive energy and sacrifice of gallant young lives may be misused to provide war lords

MAIN STREET, SALT LAKE CITY, 1936-37. (LOOKING SOUTH FROM NEAR COLLEGE AVENUE.)

A MULE DRAWN CAR FAMILIAR TO SALT LAKE CITY STREETS UNTIL LATE IN THE LAST CENTURY.

with the means to rain bombs on non-combatants!

VII.

VAST wealth invested in railroad equipment must be scrapped whenever new ideas are put into effect, but nevertheless the railroads have been increasing speed, reducing weight of carriers, and otherwise effecting economies in freight and passenger haulage. Tariffs have been generally lowered; new steam-line passenger trains have been built which in some cases weigh less than one old Pullman car; Diesel-electric and steam-electric power units have been tried in place of ponderous, old-style locomotives, and speeds of ninety to one hundred ten miles an hour have been achieved. In passenger cars many new refinements of comfort have been installed, including air-conditioning.

VIII.

SINCE the building of Dominie Peter's "Great Ship of three hundred tons burthen," which was launched at Salem, Massachusetts, in 1641, there has continued a dramatic ship-building race between the rival maritime nations, with more or less constant progress in the size and speed of vessels. But it was not until the era of steel, commencing in the nineties that really big ships could be built which could withstand the crushing blows of the great storm waves against their sides and would not break in two when poised athwart the crest of a "big one" or lying across the trough between two waves. The record for fast-sailing packets between New York and Liverpool was twenty-one days. In 1856, the *Persia*, a steamship, made the crossing from New York to Queenstown in nine days. In 1909, the *Lusitania* made the same crossing in four days, eleven hours, forty-two minutes. In 1935 the *Normandie*, 1029 feet long, 79,280 tons, crossed from New York to Land's End, 200 miles beyond Queenstown, in four days, three hours.

The modern ocean liner is really a small floating city, the last word in safe, speedy, luxurious travel. What a contrast between such majestic ships and the little old "tubs" of three-hundred-passenger capacity which carried many of the founders of Mormon families from Liverpool to New Orleans in from six weeks to two months! Each family carried its own bedding, food, and fuel for the journey, and took turns doing its own cooking. What with zeal for the Gospel and fear of the raging seas that pounded their bobbing crafts, they did so much preaching and praying on those long voyages that more than one crew, captain and all, were converted and came on with the Saints to Zion.

IX.

IN THE realm of building activity and architecture the outstanding feature of the past forty years has been the introduction of structural steel, which made possible the era of skyscrapers. There seems to be no limit to the height of these buildings, for every decade has seen them going higher and higher. The latest of these great ones is the Empire State Building of New York, twelve hundred feet high, the tallest building on earth. The modern trend in American building is in the direction of exterior simplicity of line and form and inner utility and comfort. This is particularly true in the building of houses, in which a decided revolt is noted against the jig-saw horrors of the nineteenth century and a return to the simple, unostentatious beauty of both English and Spanish colonial designs. With scientific attention to economy of space, economy of housekeeping, indoor plumbing, mechanical refrigeration, furnace heat or air-conditioning, these modern houses are very satisfactory places to live in.

This return to colonial design is significant. American colonists included many fine Old-World artisans who loved beauty and sought to plant it in the new land. But be-
(Concluded on page 726)

RAIL TRANSPORTATION DELUXE, 1937.

The OUTLAW of NAVAJO MOUNTAIN

The Story of Posey, Last Pah-Ute Outlaw

By ALBERT R. LYMAN

ONE OF OLD POSEY'S RARE AND LATER PICTURES.

THE STORY THUS FAR: Down in the wild and lawless region of Fourcorners, where Utah, Arizona, New Mexico, and Colorado come together, more than half a century ago Kit Carson rounded up the Navajos and drove them into Santa Fe, New Mexico, to keep them there in the "bullpen" for three years. While the Navajos were being thus harshly disciplined, a disaffected handful of Pah-Utes broke away from their tribe north of the San Juan River and took possession of Navajo Mountain in Navajo territory. When the Navajos came back, these Pah-Ute renegades refused to vacate the Navajo country and bad blood resulted. Sowagerie (Posey) the central character of this story was a child of one of the Pah-Ute renegades. He grew up in a cradle of anarchy. Bitseel, a son of the ousted Navajo, was Posey's most bitter enemy. In the midst of this tense situation in 1879, a colony of Mormons was sent down to settle the San Juan country, largely for the purpose of improving relationships with the Indians. Thales Haskel was their chief interpreter—a man skilled in Indian dialect and psychology. But the Navajos and Pah-Utes continued to prey upon each other and upon the Mormon settlement. During one skirmish when cowboy avengers scattered the tribe, the renegade son, Sowagerie, was momentarily separated from the tribe with Toorah, little sister of Poke, the Pah-Ute leader. This brief interlude marked the beginning of a smoldering romance that caused Sowagerie bravely to change his name to Posey and vainly dress himself in fine clothes, braid his hair, and put on war paint. This interest in his little sister, however, was relentlessly disapproved by Poke, who looked upon the "apostate" Posey as "Skunk," and so referred to him. During one period of tribal disorganization, Toorah, Posey's beloved, disappeared with her brothers, and all Posey's searchings for her were in vain. Posey finally secured vague information concerning Toorah's whereabouts, and these two lovers madly dashed to freedom. Their new found freedom together was soon interrupted, however, when Poke accidentally stumbled upon their hiding place. But he was in trouble and his ugly threatening gave way to surly compromise. Posey now entered upon the most recklessly happy part of his life. But shortly later, in an act of playfulness, occurred the greatest tragedy of Posey's life—the shooting of his beloved wife by his own hand. His unbounded sorrow was made more terrible by the avenging pursuit of Toorah's brother, Poke. But the two met under circumstances which enabled Posey to save Poke's life, whereafore Posey was relieved of further vengeance on that score by agreeing to pay a high indemnity and by agreeing to marry another of Poke's sisters—a disagreeable superannuated maiden—which circumstance began another career of heckling evil. Later a handful of Mormon settlers from Bluff captured Posey in a humiliating manner, put him in irons and brought him before a justice of the peace, where he was bound over to appear at the next session of the district court. By a ruse Posey later escaped and went into exile at Navajo Mountain. He was shaken by his first personal experience with white man's justice and sent word to the inhabitants of Bluff, asking their forgiveness and pledging to mend his ways. The charges were withdrawn and Posey returned to the community on temporary good behavior. But as the terror of his exile began to fade, the humiliation of it loomed greater in his mind, and he took steps to see that it would not happen again by going to Colorado to purchase a long range

gun, and by learning how the recently installed telephones could be used and how communities could be separated by cutting wires. Thus prepared, he returned to his old ways with a vengeance. In the midst of this situation Poke's son, Tse-ne-gat, was accused of robbing and killing a sheepherder. Peace officers came to arrest him. In the skirmish that followed, both Pah-Utes and whites were killed. Posey had treacherously used a flag of truce to protect himself while he gained shooting position. General Hugh L. Scott was sent out from Washington to represent the government in this tragedy. Poke, Posey, Tse-ne-gat, and Jess Posey were taken to Denver for trial. Royally treated and exonerated, they were released by the government and sent home. This generous treatment they interpreted as an act of weakness, and began to plan further misdeeds. With an increasing belief in his own immunity from all punishment, Posey acquired another long range gun, traveled a long distance to purchase a horse that was superior to anything in the San Juan region, and in other ways prepared for the inevitable conflict that was destined to come. His preparations, however, were interrupted by another gambling affray with Bitseel in which Posey's prize horse was involved and from which he extricated himself by striking Bitseel with the butt of a revolver and dashing for freedom—thus postponing another final meeting. The October installment describes Posey's activities in organizing and firing to violence the hoodlum element of the tribe—an element, which having been inspired to violence proved embarrassingly difficult even for Posey to control. Finally Pahneab, a young leader of the hoodlum element, was arrested with Dutchie's boy and brought to trial for holding up a sheepherder at gun's point. Posey entered the schoolhouse courtroom and during the noon recess aided the defendants to break for liberty, with Sheriff Oliver in full pursuit.*

CHAPTER XIX—THE BIG STIR

THE BIG stir was on! It had come as the sharp crack of a whip, and it found most of the Pah-Utes lounging around the stores or killing time at other places in town. Many of them knew nothing even yet of what had happened.

When Posey and *Dutchie-toats* (Dutchie's boy) ran panting into camp, everything was in an uproar at once. Pahneab had dashed by on the black mare and was bringing the horses from the sagebrush flat beyond. They must be gone! No time to lose. Posey dared now to give imperious orders. But most of their people loafed stupidly somewhere in town. Parts of families were at the *wickiups* fumed and cried for children or wives or fathers or brothers still in Blanding. Oliver had turned back from the edge of the trees, but he would get help and be after them.

Then some of their people arrived breathless from town,—wild, terrified. They reported that every white man in Blanding was running for his gun—getting horses to ride —any horses in sight, the very first they could find.

Pahneab came pell-mell with the ponies from the flat, and everybody in camp ran to get his rope on his animals to pack up and be gone. Teegre sprang to the back of his buckskin and raced away to the east rim of West Water at the edge of town where he called in long and penetrating tones to his people, *"Whoo-eeh-eeh! Tos-pon pikey! Tooish apane!"* His magnificent voice carried far through the cool spring air, but his people in town, though they heard, had been hurriedly rounded up by determined men who ordered them not to move a foot.

As Teegre returned on the keen jump, Joe Bishop, heavy, perspiring, and panting from undue haste came dragging up from West Water. He said he was the last man to escape the roundup and get out of town; fifty or more of their people were prisoners—men standing over them with guns. No use to wait longer for them.

Impotent haste and frightened confusion reigned in camp. They cinched saddles on squirming, protesting cayuses; they piled beds and provisions and supplies on the saddles in bunglesome heaps. They urged their motley flocks of goats up from the groves of oak in the canyon, expecting every minute to be attacked by the men from the town.

They must be off. *"Tooish apane! Tooish apane!"* commanded the general impatiently.

But how could they start on The Old Trail with nearly half their people held as prisoners in town to become possible hostages pending the outcome of the trouble? No difference—they must go. Posey would come back in the night and get the prisoners—it was a promise—*"Tooish apane!"*

They mounted in a panic of suspense and headed wildly for the nearest cover of thick trees and rocks to the south. Joe Bishop, puffing and palpitating with his fat and trying to get his saddle on his fidgety pony, was left behind. He hadn't got the blamed thing in place when Bill Oliver and half a dozen armed men rode into camp.

"Where's your boy?" demanded the sheriff.

"I show you." Old Joe panted,

JESS POSEY, SON OF OLD POSEY

getting his ponderous weight in the saddle, and starting on the reeking trail of the goats and the ponies, the white men at his heels.

Pahneab's father had no intention of giving his son away. He figured that once among the thick trees he could dodge out of sight, and hurrying forward to his people he could tell them who and how many were in pursuit. But when he dodged, Dave Black dodged after him, and Dave had to jab him fiercely in the ribs with the muzzle of his gun to convince him the only way to save his life was to go back with Black to the roundup in town.

Three miles down West Water Point, Posey and his fugitives stopped behind a barrier of big rocks to consider. Which way should they go, and at what point should they enter The Big Trail? The Big Trail was to the west, and the general wanted to turn that way at once. He was met again by the popular howl about the people held as prisoners in town. The best fighters of the tribe were there, Scotty among them. And they should by all means have Poke to be their leader.

Poke for their leader! The idea! After all Posey had done! His blood boiled.

And the inevitable second wife was with the popular majority, making a veiled threat of what her brother would do if he were left out. Also, a-plenty would happen to them if they went without him, even if he did nothing. They lacked little of open mutiny right there and then.

Posey knew they must go on in spite of everything; they must go even if he had to yield a point; and he did yield a very dear point, almost amounting to the abdication of his imperial ambition. He sent a messenger telling Poke to meet them, and then instead of getting off to the west nearer the Old Trail, they had to turn east to meet the old bear at Recapture.

Posey wanted very much to have Poke with them, but not to supersede him. He knew that one grunt from the old grizzly was worth more than forty fighting men, but Posey had a more cherished reason than that for wanting the old cavalier in the ranks of the big stir.

Poke, more than any other man in the tribe had been the author of all the big fights hitherto, and Posey had got a place in them only by inviting himself, and then he had to march in the mean tail of the parade. Now, as the prime mover of this big event, he had a great ambition to invite the old bear to occupy a place in the ranks behind him.

Yet, after this mutinous display, with half his people under arrest, and the second wife carrying on as terribly as a hen with one chicken, he would be delighted to have the old grizzly take the whole infernal mess off his hands. As the brains of three riproaring wars, and with at least seven dead men to his credit, Poke could paw this mutinous herd into line and compel every man to do his ragged best.

The messenger left at once for Yellow Jacket, leaning forward on his speeding horse, and the outfit pushed on towards Recapture. Late in the afternoon they stopped to take a much needed lunch at the old cabin on Murphy Point.

In ten minutes Sheriff Oliver and his little posse appeared at the field gate to the north of them. The posse was rather too far away for a shot, but Posey plowed up the dust in front of them as a gentle hint to wait a little while. The Pah-Utes behind the cabin rushed their re-

(Continued on page 714)

THE FOUR PRESIDENTS OF THE CHURCH UNDER WHOSE ADMINISTRATIONS "THE IMPROVEMENT ERA" HAS CONTINUED ITS CHURCH-WIDE MISSION; LEFT TO RIGHT: WILFORD WOODRUFF, LORENZO SNOW, JOSEPH F. SMITH, AND HEBER J. GRANT.

40 YEARS of SERVICE

By HARRISO   R. MERRILL

Director, Extension Division, B. Y. U., Member of the General Board of the Y. M. M. I. A., and Former Managing Editor of "The Improvement Era."

WHEN this number of *The Improvement Era* reaches the hands of its readers in all parts of the world, the magazine will be successfully launched upon its forty-first year of service, for November is the birthday month of the publication which, for forty years, has been near and dear to hundreds of thousands of Latter-day Saints in all the world.

Though the magazine has been a constant, steady, hopeful, courageous, and inspiring voice in a changing and often muddled and darkened world, if Professor Pitkin's famous statement, "Life begins at forty," is true, then this number launches the magazine upon a career that will far transcend that of the past forty years, glorious as that has been.

From a tiny infant without ancestors, unless the old *Contributor* could be called an ancestor, born

STARTED WITHOUT CAPITAL AT A TIME WHEN THE CHURCH WAS IN DEEP FINANCIAL DESPAIR. "THE IMPROVEMENT ERA" HAS SERVED A GROWING WORLD-WIDE ORGANIZATION DURING THE ADMINISTRATIONS OF FOUR PRESIDENTS OF THE CHURCH.

THROUGH FOUR STORMY DECADES THE "ERA HAS SOUNDED A SAFE COURSE.

during the Pioneer Jubilee year, the magazine has grown to be a fully developed, mature, dignified, and much-loved adult in the prime of life and service. Nurtured and loved and watched over by some of the best and ablest leaders of the Church, it has become an influential organ with an important message for all the world, and due to continued effort of those who have had its destinies in charge, it is taking that message to all the world. There

is scarcely a nation or a people or an island of the sea that is not visited by this bearer of truth and good tidings.

It is of more than passing interest, really of great significance, that there is one man who has been closely identified with the magazine

PAST EDITORS AND ASSOCIATE EDITORS OF "THE IMPROVEMENT ERA," LEFT TO RIGHT: JOSEPH F. SMITH, B. H. ROBERTS, EDWARD H. ANDERSON, HUGH J. CANNON, ELSIE TALMAGE BRANDLEY, HARRISON R. MERRILL.

PAST BUSINESS MANAGERS AND ASSISTANTS: HEBER J. GRANT, THOMAS HULL, ALPHA J. HIGGS, MORONI SNOW, MELVIN J. BALLARD, O. B. PETERSON.

since the beginning. It was largely owing to his force and drive that the *Era* was born at all and that it has continued to grow in the face of many difficulties. That man is President Heber J. Grant, first business manager and present senior editor.

Forty years ago when the magazine was without funds and when there were no funds to be had from the Church, which was then in dire financial distress, President Grant was made business manager. His zeal carried him into all parts of the Church and there he preached *Improvement Era*. Thousands have heard him tell, in a semi-serious and semi-humorous manner, many of the experiences which were his during those early years of desperate struggle for existence.

The magazine has lived during the administrations of four presi-

M. I. A. HEADS UNDER WHOSE ADMINISTRATIONS THE "ERA" HAS BEEN PUBLISHED. LEFT TO RIGHT, FIRST ROW: WILFORD WOODRUFF, LORENZO SNOW, JOSEPH F. SMITH, ANTHONY W. IVINS; SECOND ROW: GEORGE ALBERT SMITH, RUTH MAY FOX (Y. W. M. I. A.), ALBERT E. BOWEN, AND GEORGE Q. MORRIS.

dents of the Church. Begun in 1897, when President Wilford Woodruff was Trustee-in-Trust, it has continued through the administrations of Presidents Lorenzo Snow and Joseph F. Smith, and for nearly nineteen years during the administration of President Heber J. Grant. During all of that time, President Grant has been either business manager or editor of the magazine, which is as dear to him as a living personality.

He held the position of manager until the death of President Joseph F. Smith, when he was made editor-in-chief with Edward H. Anderson as assistant and with Melvin J. Ballard as business manager. And the editor's chair he still dignifies.

The history of *The Improvement Era* is a story of faith and works united in a most efficient manner. *The Contributor*, a magazine which had been in circulation among the Saints for seventeen years, was discontinued in the fall of 1896, for lack of support, leaving the Church with no magazine through which the young men could be effectively reached. This loss was soon keenly felt. President Grant writes:

Twice in my life I prayed to the Lord to

be appointed to a position. The first time was when there was a disorganization of the general superintendency of the Mutual Improvement Associations because of the failure of one of the men in that superintendency to retain his standing in one of the

A MINIATURE COVER REPRODUCTION OF VOLUME I, NUMBER I.

high positions in the Church. I got down on my knees and I asked the Lord to call me to be one of the superintendency of the Young Men's Mutual Improvement Association. The *Contributor* was a very splendid magazine, one of the very finest magazines the Church has published. . . . It had died a natural death because of the lack of support on the part of the people. We had no magazine, and there were no meetings of the general board, except that they met once in about every six months. I realized that they ought to meet every week, that they should come together and converse and work out programs. I prayed to the Lord that I might be chosen as one of the general superintendency. The very next day when I was in the president's office, President Joseph F. Smith said to President Woodruff who was then also General Superintendent of the Y. M. M. I. A.: "Brother Woodruff, I believe you ought to have two other counselors in the superintendency of the Young Men's Mutual. I suggest that Brother Grant here and Brother B. H. Roberts be counselors as well as myself." . . . We immediately called a meeting and we considered the proposition of starting *The Improvement Era*. . . .

At that time, the Church was in debt and without credit, and almost

at its lowest ebb financially. No
funds were available for such a
project, the committee was informed by the office of the Trustee-in-
Trust. However, plans were formu-
lated in the late summer of 1897 for
launching a magazine. Said President Roberts in an account he wrote
of the matter, twenty-eight years
later:

The strong assertion that those who supposed that we had no capital with which
to begin the publication of the organ for
the Young Men's Mutual Improvement
Association were entirely mistaken. Our
capital was the interest of the young men
of the Church of Jesus Christ of Latter-day
Saints in the Mutual cause; and that had

FIRST HOME OF THE
"ERA", TEMPLETON
BUILDING, SOUTH
TEMPLE AND MAIN
STREETS, SALT LAKE
CITY.

only to be appealed to and drawn upon
in order to be sufficient and permanent in
the maintenance of the Young Men's organ. It was urged with complete confidence that if our case were fittingly presented to the young men of the Church,
and our determination to publish such an
organ was strong enough, that we could
supply the capital by asking our young
men for a one year's subscription to the
magazine, strictly in advance, and before
any numbers were printed at all. . . .

That was rather a unique plan for raising capital, and many were the predictions
of failure should we attempt to execute it!
But the committee in charge were then
young men, and represented at that time
the spirit of faith and confidence in things
undertaken, characteristic of the young
men of the Church; and so the plan, with
some misgiving, was assented to, and a
campaign for raising the capital was
planned.

The general outline of that plan, as I
recall it, was first of all to adopt a name,
have the management and editorial staff
appointed, and then send out campaigning
companies into all the territory occupied
by the Church organizations to solicit subscriptions. The business management was
placed in the capable and enthusiastic hands
of Heber J. Grant, as manager, with Thomas Hull, assistant, and the editors were an-

nounced as Joseph F. Smith and B. H.
Roberts.

A T THAT early time, before a single
magazine was printed, the subscription price was set at two dollars a year. Several members of
the General Board at that time were
also members of the Council of the
Twelve and the First Council of
the Seventy; they took the matter up in quarterly conferences
which they attended and in other
ways assisted the campaign. Though

President Roberts could not remember the number or the personnel of
all the campaigning companies, he
has left us a delightful paragraph
or two telling of the activities of his
own company. He says:

The company of canvassers with which
the writer was associated was assigned a
group of counties in northern Utah and
southern Idaho, and their tour occupied
something more than a month or six weeks
and was somewhat typical of other groups
who went upon the same mission.

Our territory consisted of the Afton

Y. M. M. I. A. COMMITTEE WHO PLANNED THE PRESENT ENLARGED "ERA". LEFT TO RIGHT: GEORGE Q. MORRIS, CHAIRMAN; JOHN D. GILES, STRINGAM A. STEVENS.

Stake, in Wyoming, Bear Lake and Oneida Stakes, Idaho, and Cache Stake, Utah.

The personnel of our party consisted of the late Robert Easton, and his wife Jeanette Young Easton, Thomas Hull and his wife Margaret Hull, Douglas M. Todd, Viola Pratt Gillett and her mother, Mrs.

RIGHT: ANOTHER OF THE HOMES OF "THE IMPROVEMENT ERA," 47 EAST SO. TEMPLE, SALT LAKE CITY.
Photo by D. F. Davis.

Milando Pratt, Walter S. Lamoreaux, and myself. Those who are acquainted with the personnel of this company will at once surmise that it was strong for its singing talent, especially in the personages of "Bob" Easton, Viola Pratt Gillett, Mrs. Margaret Hull, and Mr. Lamoreaux. They were to give concerts and the rest of us were to represent the prose proposition of raising the Era's capital. . . .

Easton and his associate singers were

LEFT: PRESENT HOME OF "THE IMPROVEMENT ERA," 50 NORTH MAIN STREET, SALT LAKE CITY.
Photo by Homer Wakefield.

at their best. Something in the outdoor life, and meeting in the homes, seemed to give a touch of romance to our undertaking. Everyone was cheerful, and we often went serenading people in their homes in out-of-the-way places. There "Bob" Easton, in Scotch songs, and Viola Pratt Gillett, in sentimental ones, with solos by Sister Hull, and duets and trios thrown in for good measure, in which Lamoreaux joined, together with choruses and hymns

in which Hull and myself sometimes swelled the chorus, seemed to be taken as currency for the large draughts of buttermilk and lunches our company consumed.

Everywhere our public meetings were well attended, subscriptions for the forthcoming magazine rolled up on every hand. In other parts of the Church territory, as well as in ours, the young men of Israel everywhere responded to this appeal, and became the *capital*, the only capital with which the magazine started.

But despite this loyal and ready

response, the financing and business management of *The Improvement Era* continued to be a burdensome task, and President Grant began a campaign of solicitation by personal letter for subscribers and donors. In this activity he used his energies and his private means, and the energies of his family. His home, then on Second East Street in Salt Lake City, was ofttimes converted into a veritable mailing room, with the President's children folding and sealing while he signed thousands of letters.

(Continued on page 720)

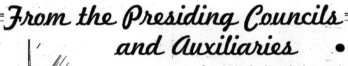

From the Presiding Councils and Auxiliaries

Its arrival in far-distant lands is eagerly watched for.

It·is clean, it is wholesome, it is refreshing,·and a delight·to its thousands of subscribers.

The First Council of The Seventy,
By *Rufus K. Hardy.*

———

Two score years of splendid service in the presentation of interesting and instructive subjects, beginning with the jubilee year of this Commonwealth, justifies most cordial felicitations to this important magazine and to all who have contributed to its success.

We honor especially an outstanding character—the first Business Manager and present Editor-in-Chief and President of the Church, Heber J. Grant.

His courage and persistence, his generosity and enthusiasm have been large factors in carrying forward this publication in the trying days of its early existence.

May this magazine continue its outstanding career!

The Presiding Bishopric,
By *Sylvester Q. Cannon.*

It gives the Relief Society great pleasure to extend congratulations to *The Improvement Era* on the fortieth anniversary of its founding. It is impossible to estimate the power for good it has been among the people; a source of enlightenment and of entertainment.

* * *

At this interesting period, may the thought be expressed, that the sympathetic understanding of the needs of the hour, the vision, courage and faith of the past, continue to direct its course for the next forty years.

General Board of Relief Society,
By *Louise Y. Robison.*

———

The Deseret Sunday School Union in its 89th year, applauds *The Improvement Era* for its 40 illustrious years of building faith and fervor into the characters of Latter-day Saints. It is a glorious record for your magazine. So long as such excellence marks your performance, we shall be cheering for you.

Cordially yours,
Geo. D. Pyper,
Milton Bennion,
Geo. R. Hill, Jr.
General Superintendency.

A magazine is successful in proportion to the friends it makes. *The Improvement Era* numbers its friends in the thousands because of its inspiring, enlightening, and helpful messages. The Primary Association is happy to be numbered among its admiring friends and takes pleasure in extending congratulations and abundant good wishes for its continued success.

The General Board of the
Primary Association.

The Improvement Era is to be congratulated, after forty years, on its fine appearance. Indeed, it is so bright and attractive that one is tempted, no matter how busy he may be, to pause and investigate. Opening the magazine and turning to the title page his eye would immediately catch this extraordinary line: "The Glory of God Is Intelligence."

And glancing over the . . . contents and . . . finding them to be of the very highest character he would be led to exclaim, "Now I know why *The Improvement Era* is so widely read and so popular throughout ·the Church, and even beyond its borders."

The investigator would not be long in discovering that the editorials written by President Heber J. Grant and John A. Widtsoe, Editors; Richard L. Evans, Managing Editor, and Marba C. Josephson, Associate Editor, add interest and strength to this important magazine. The ultimate success of a publication depends in part upon the general management. In the management of the *Era* the investigator would recognize the splendid work·being done by George Q. Morris, General Manager; Clarissa A. Beesley, Associate Manager; and J. K. Orton, Business Manager.

May signal success attend the coming forth each month of *The Improvement Era,* is the ardent wish of

The Council of the Twelve.
By *Rudger Clawson, President.*

We desire to congratulate the Era upon its forty years of successful achievement.

A thing well born is well on its way to success. Its impetus has never diminished since its founder and business manager, President Heber J. Grant, and its first editor, President Joseph F. Smith, launched it forth on its errand of home educational enlightenment and its missionary career.

Being in touch with the missionary activities of the Church, we can truthfully say that the *Era* is and has been a messenger of joy, peace, and comfort to the missionaries in the field and the disseminator of the Latter-day Gospel truths to many not yet of our faith.

TWO
BROTHERS

A SHORT SHORT
STORY OF THE
ETERNAL CONFLICT

BY

HELEN TENNA TYREE

RAIN and mud. Mud and rain. Sorrow and dread and futility. Men with courage and men with fear. So this was the front!

My sensations on going over the top? At first I thought of home. Pastel skies, cool mountains, green fields. Then—into a hell of ricocheting lead! A symphony of death! The battlefield was a tumbled chaos of broken bodies. Dismembered souls drifted in the cannon smoke. Chatter . . . chatter . . . an unending rhythm—was that machine guns or my teeth chattering? Some of the boys ran ahead of me. The mowing got them—over like wheat they went—sliced off—quick—easy. My feet snagged on bodies. I kept on going. No telling—I might be next.

What an experience! My mind said that several times, I remember. But my body was numb, drenched, cold. And the senselessness of it all pounded at me.

A man fell in my way. Did it hurt much? I wondered. His eyes closed so quietly.

All around the air surcharged with death—with transient life. Hate crescendoing in song — bursting in screeching splendor. Shells—screaming—spiraling! Flash! Flame! Eternity swooping upon me with a thousand stars!

That smothering sense of death was hushing my throat. I fought. I wouldn't die! But I was so tired. I almost wanted to die.

I was drifting. Rising and sinking—just as someone is said to feel with a shot of morphine.

Here's what happened. You can make what you will of it.

I *know*. I know I passed into that mysterious half-realm between life and death. There perception is keener—there we see the ordinarily unseen—we hear the ordinarily unheard! There we are sensitized to vibrations on a higher plane than those of earth. Delirious? Oh, no! My mind was clearer than crystal!

I could feel someone standing there. Finally I opened my eyes. I could see someone in white and someone garbed in black. Out of the haze two faces were materializing. The mists cleared. One was radiant . . . light. The other dark . . . haunted. I knew them some-

how. Where had I seen them before? I kept trying to remember. They say I was shell-shocked. But I tell you I saw through space and time!

Those two surely resembled one another, I thought. They looked like brothers—but separated by different worlds! Suddenly they became aware of one another. They did not speak. The one in white stretched out his hand. But the dark one stood sullen. He didn't appear to notice the outstretched hand. A fleeting look of pain came over the dark face and then a sneer.

They were like people who have been separated for a long time and find words painful. They just stood and looked at each other. It got on my nerves, the way they kept standing there. Silent. Death-like. The dark one kept on trying to sneer, but there was a heart-broken look about him—like someone forever doomed—someone forever lost . . . lost in a world of nameless shadows and horror! I felt sorry for him. He turned to go.

The other stopped him. . .

"So—we meet again, my brother!" There was the gentleness of prayer in that voice. "It's been a long time."

Still the dark one didn't answer.

"My brother!" the shining one had said—and into the sweet sternness of his face came deep sorrow.

My brother! My brother! How those words sobbed themselves into my heart and chanted in my soul! And then I remembered who they were. Spiritual memories stirred in me.

. . . Existence was new. The universe was young. I heard again a crucified voice breaking in anguish. Again I heard a father's tortured words ringing into the stillness of eternity: "Lucifer! Lucifer! Why hast thou fallen, Son of the Morning?"

I sensed the half-turning of that soul moved by this omnipotent eloquence. Then sullen pride triumphed. That god-like but self-destroying pride! I sensed the perverted glory of that lost son. He who had been among the most exalted—falling—falling from the grace of God!

DESPAIR weighed me! How could we—lesser ones—hope to prevail when such greatness had failed? He—the Son of the Morning!

Voices murmured. Awe crept over all.

And then he was gone—the Prince of Darkness wearing his defeat majestically. I will never forget that terrible, tragic deserter! Alone — unwanted — but not unmourned. . . .

And now the brothers had met again.

(Concluded on page 707)

683

...OF VISION

STARTED BY SUSA YOUNG GATES IN 1889 AND EDITED BY EIGHT WOMEN OF VISION, THE "YOUNG WOMAN'S JOURNAL" IN ITS FORTIETH YEAR IN 1929 MERGED WITH "THE IMPROVEMENT ERA."

By MARBA C. JOSEPHSON

Associate Editor of "The Improvement Era"

SUSA YOUNG GATES
(Founder of the "Young
Woman's Journal" and
Editor, 1889-1901.)

BEHIND every great movement stands a great person, one who towers above his fellows and whose shadow elongates to mold events and shape destiny. The story behind the founding of the *Young Woman's Journal* is poignantly bound up in the life of one whose vision and care brought the *Journal* through its perilous years of early childhood. Eight other great women also figured in its growth. Their genius nurtured the *Journal* into maturity and all of them lived to see this child of their hopes safely embarked on a greater journey when, as it reached its maturity of forty years, it combined with *The Improvement Era*.

We are told in the Doctrine and Covenants: "To every man is given a gift by the Spirit of God. To some is given one, and to some is given another, that all may be profited thereby." Each of the women who fostered the *Journal* had rich gifts. But of necessity the story of the woman whose vision inspired its founding must receive the greatest consideration in any article dealing with that magazine.

While nothing is said in the Doctrine and Covenants about women's having gifts, many of them did, some of them by virtue of the men who fathered them. One such woman was Susa Young Gates, daughter of Brigham Young by Lucy Bigelow, who also by right of descent was entitled to many gifts of the spirit.

One of the surprising things about our early Mormon women and their descendants was their ability to see into the deeper significance of life and in spite of hard times keep bright the flame of desire for the

good things, both for themselves and others of their faith. Theirs was an entirely unselfish devotion to the cause of the majority. They knew that their personal accomplishments might carry them far, but they forgot self entirely for the benefit of the greater number.

Susa Young Gates, born of a generation who had conquered dis-

MAY BOOTH TALMAGE
(Editor, 1901-1902.)

tance, entered a new pioneering field. Brilliant, friendly, capable, she could have gone far in her own right. But first and last, she was a Latter-day Saint; all else must be subservient to her wish to be a good Latter-day Saint.

ANN M. CANNON
(Editor, 1902-1907.)

To read the accomplishments of Sister Gates sounds incredible to those who did not come in personal contact with this vital, tireless woman. The number of "firsts" to her credit is amazing. She started life with a first, since, although she was not the first child of Brigham Young, she was the first child born in the historic Lion House on March 18, 1856.

When she was attending school at the University of Utah, Dr. Park appointed her associate editor of the

WITH the celebration of the fortieth year of the initial publication of "The Improvement Era," it is only fitting that recognition be accorded a magazine which submerged its identity in order to make a greater magazine for the Church. That magazine, "The Young Woman's Journal," owed much to the far-seeing women who piloted it through its perilous early life. They too must share in the glory that has accrued to the magazine which has resulted from their uniting to make a greater "Improvement Era."

first western college paper, *The College Lantern*. In 1870, when President Young moved her mother's family to St. George, Utah, she organized a large club of men and women, called the Union Club. 1878, when she was in Provo, she organized the music department at B. Y. U. In 1897, she organized the domestic science department at the same institution. Sister Gates was also organizer of the first state chapter in Utah of the Daughters of the Revolution.

All of these activities show the tremendous energy, vision, and abilities of this truly remarkable woman whose greatness was recognized among women outside of Utah. Susan B. Anthony upon one occasion

ELEN WALLACE
(Associate Editor, 1902-1907.)

684

said to her that she would make Sister Gates president of the National Council of Women, if she would forget her militant Mormonism. Sister Gates replied characteristically that the price was too high.

A woman's first duty according to Latter-day Saints is, whenever possible, to rear children under the everlasting covenant, according to the eternal family plan. Although tragedy stalked Sister Gates in her desire to live this law, she rose above her sorrow and finally earned the merited satisfaction of having a large and gifted family. Her first obedience was always to the Priesthood and when her husband, Jacob F. Gates, was called to fill a mission to the Sandwich Islands, as the Hawaiian Islands were then called, she unquestioningly accompanied him and three of their children were born there. Had not her father led a people into the wilderness? She, a daughter of that father, could do no less than accompany her husband on his special appointment.

Proof of her undying love of the Church and devotion for its principles is manifested in her sacrifice of her own career in order to become a mother in Israel. In addition to the thirteen children whom she bore, she became a light to countless children not her own, who lovingly called her "Aunt Susa."

She herself never felt that she had sacrificed. On one occasion at least, she said: "It was better that I marry and give of my talent to my children. If I had continued with my own career, there would have been only one. Because I married, one daughter has achieved international fame with her golden voice; one son has given his musical talent to the Church; another son has become recognized in the field of literature; another daughter has become well-known in domestic science."

NATURALLY, when a woman of the ability, the spirituality, the geniality which Sister Gates possessed, turned her attention to any field, she was certain to meet success. When, accordingly, while still in the Islands, she had the vision of what a

ELSIE TALMAGE
BRANDLEY
(Associate Editor, 1923-
1929; Editor, 1929.)

magazine for young women could mean to them and to the Church, she was not long in trying to realize the dream. In this instance, she once again proved her willingness to obey and follow the counsel of the Priesthood. While there were already three Church publications: the *Juvenile Instructor*, for the Sunday School; the *Woman's Exponent*, for the Relief Society; and the *Contributor*, for the Young Men's Association; there was no magazine for the young women. There was no opportunity for the young women of the Church to receive special messages, to voice their opinions, or to

MARY CONNELLY
KIMBALL
(Editor, 1907-1923.)

ask questions. She wrote first of all to Joseph F. Smith, second counselor to President Wilford Woodruff, and explained the plan for this new magazine. He advised her to counsel with President Woodruff, which she did. With his approval and recommendation, she wrote to the presidency of the Young Ladies'

CLARISSA A. BEESLEY
(Associate Editor, 1914-
1923; Editor, 1923-
1929.)

Mutual Improvement Association, who voted in favor of the publication and presented their wishes to the First Presidency.

In May, 1889, when the Gates family returned from their mission, the work began. In October, 1889, the first issue was published. Two aims were ever-present in the mind of Sister Gates and her co-workers: 1, the spirit of the magazine should take precedence over literary forms; 2, home writers should be encouraged in order to cultivate talent among our own people. In the pages of the magazine were such departments as: House and Home, Dress Department, Health and Hygiene, Our Girls' Department. In addition were to be found fiction, poetry, and articles on literary appreciation.

Of course, the financial situation

ESTELLE NEFF
CALDWELL
(Co-editor with Elen
Wallace, 1905.)

was serious. The only way of advertising was by word of mouth. Many of the women, including Sister Gates' own mother, paid all of their own expenses and drove their own horses and buggies into the outlying districts that the magazine might continue.

For eleven years, Sister Gates was the guiding spirit of the *Journal*. Traveling back and forth from her home in Provo, she was ever at the helm. Her keen intellect, her warm sympathies, her intense vitality kept the new magazine going.

When her husband was called on another mission, this time to New York, "Aunt Susa" resigned the editorship so that she might accompany him. Her indomitable spirit which had kept the magazine going during its eleven hazardous years was sufficient to carry it forward through the succeeding years.

Her courage in face of disaster, her sublime faith can best be illustrated in episodes from her life, many of which have been a constant source of encouragement to those who have known of them. After the tragic death of a little daughter, instead of futilely weeping, Sister Gates went home and canned tomatoes. Her heart ached, as all women's hearts must ache in the face of a loss so intense, but hers was the truly valiant spirit. She would work out her grief rather than succumb to it. She early in her life learned the value of true prayer. Whenever things seemed too hard to bear, she went to the Lord. She talked the situation through with Him. Then when she arose from her knees, she left her sorrow and heartbreak with Him. She carried hope and courage to her new tasks.

Susa Young Gates had a talent, recognized it, and acted on it. From her vision, the *Young Woman's Journal* received the impetus to go forward through exactly forty years of existence under eight capable editors before it was wedded to *The Improvement Era*. The magazine began with the first issue in October, 1889, and closed with its final issue in October, 1929—forty years of glorious achievement.

Ensign Challenges

"IN HONOR OF THE ERA'S FORTIETH ANNIVERSARY AND PRESIDENT GRANT'S FORTY YEARS' SERVICE TO THE ERA, AT LEAST FORTY PER CENT OF ALL OUR HOMES WILL HAVE THE CHURCH MAGAZINE."

ALLENGE in the Church-wide campaign place *The Improvement Era* in every ae has been issued by Ensign Stake, last ·d place winner in Class B Stakes for ›er of subscriptions. One of the larger he Church, Ensign has set its immediate 250 subscriptions—40 per cent of the ›mes in the stake—and has coupled this ›jective of a new all-time Church-wide h a further expressed determination to symbolism of its name and be an Ensign ırch.

sign stake *Era* objective for the current n it several points of particular signifi- ddition to the fact that it represents 40 Ensign Stake Church homes. The goal l at this figure to commemorate *The Im- Era's* forty years' service to the Church ient Grant's forty years' service to the : objective has also been established to sident Grant, founder and editor of the ı eighty-first birthday anniversary, which the same month as the *Era's* fortieth y—November, 1937.

sign Stake plan, which involves many ıtures, was launched several weeks ago Smith and Chet Larson, Ensign Directors, who have lined up behind ıctive and loyal support of the stake and , A. leaders; George Cannon Young and Clawson, stake M. I. A. superintendent ent; and the stake presidency, Winslow George J. Cannon, and Oscar W. Mc- ıd the bishops of wards.

ıl meeting of the stake presidency, stake cil, stake M. I. A. leaders, and ward was called early in September to approve h the plan, which provides for the ap- f an *Era* chairman by the bishop of each for the appointment of captains of fifty m as many *Era* workers as are necessary ıted to visit twelve families each.

cards were shown at the Ensign stake convention at which High Councilman l sounded the challenge. These placards shown also at other stake and ward Some of them read as follows:

Onward with the Church—The *Era* will keep you Informed.

The *Era*—40 Years of Successful Missionary Work.

The *Era* Tells the Church about the Church.

In the *Era*—Messages from the First Presidency.

The *Era* Read in Every Home.

Ensign Stake Goal—1250.

Ensign Stake to Lead the Church—Subscribers and Readers.

The *Era* is the Organ of the Priesthood Quorums.

IT IS peculiarly fitting that Ensign stake should undertake to set a new all-time Church-wide *Era* record in this fortieth anniversary year be- cause it is President Grant's home stake.

It is not thought, however, that Ensign's earnest and spectacular challenge will be left uncontested. Most of last year's leading stakes have declared themselves out for this year's high percentage or high numbers placements and most of the stakes who did not place among the leaders last year are organized for higher records this year. Last year's record by Salt Lake and Ensign stakes has spurred other Salt Lake City stakes to project their activi- ties for greater accomplishment. Brother and Sister W. H. Earnshaw who directed Salt Lake Stake's outstanding achievement last year are again directing the program in that stake. President Leo J. Muir, Superintendent George A. Baker, President Geneva Langlois, and Arnold G. Morris, *Era* Director, who were behind last year's all-time all-Church record in Los Angeles, also have plans for this year, and Stake President H. R. Price has already set Maricopa stake's goal at 1000 *Era* subscriptions.

But above all the friendly and interesting stake competition and challenge and·counter-challenge is the great motivating purpose of service and missionary endeavor—the determination and desire to comply with the oft-repeated request. of the President ·of the Church to place the *Era*, the Church-wide missionary, in every home in order that a growing and spreading world-wide Church may be kept in touch with its leaders and with each other, in order that wholesome and informative Church reading matter may have its influence in every home, and·in order that the Church may be kept closely united in a restless and shifting world.—*R. L. E.*

A GOOD INVESTMENT

A SHORT SHORT STORY

BY

GILBERT H.
ANDREWS

"MOTHER!", ten-year-old Johnny stopped eating his cereal for a minute, "What is a good investment?"

"Whatever put that idea into your head, son?"

"Well, I heard you and Daddy talking after he came from meeting last night. He said the reason he promised to give five hundred dollars to the new meetinghouse was because he thought it would be a good investment. What did he mean?"

"Well, dear, a good investment means that you put your money into something that pays. That is, you get back enough to pay for what you put in and more."

"Does that mean that if we put that much money into the ward chapel we'll get our money back some time?"

"No, we probably won't get our money back; but there are other things we could get out of it that would be even more valuable. But if you don't hurry you'll be late for school."

Johnny wondered what they could get out of a new meetinghouse that would be worth more than money. Goodness knows they had a hard time getting enough to live on as it was. There was the new stove Mother had planned on. It cost only about a hundred, and they had waited a long time trying to save enough to buy it. And now they wouldn't get it for a long time yet. He had heard them say last night that they would have to give it up.

It seemed to Johnny that mother needed a stove worse than almost anything. That one in the kitchen caused no end of trouble. And after all, a ward chapel wasn't used much except on Sunday. Money and furniture around the house were used every day. A stove was not all they needed. Other folks had new ice boxes that even froze ice cream and kept things cool—but mother kept her things cool in the ditch behind the house.

Everybody seemed thrilled over the new chapel. Johnny was proud of the fact that he was one of the first group of Deacons that were called to the stand and presented to the people. He noticed that his father and mother seemed proud of him as he stood there before the congregation.

The new building was grand. They never had to dismiss some

of the Sunday School classes now on account of cold weather. But he'd had a lot of fun in the old one —been scared, too! There was the time the President of the Primary had asked him to lead in prayer. She had stood by his side with her arm around him and helped. It seemed a little thing now, but he'd been mighty proud after it was over.

When he became a Scout he passed most of his tests and received most of his badges in the new chapel. He was ordained a Teacher and then a Priest there. First time he helped with the Sacrament he thought he knew the blessing on the bread, and, when he was half way through, he had to stop and start over with a card in front of him.

Shortly after he was ordained an Elder he was called on a mission. They had a party for him in the new chapel and almost everyone in the ward seemed to be there to help show him a good time. It made him feel more important, like somehow the ward was part his.

WHEN he first landed in the mission field, the outlook wasn't so bright. How in the world could he ever learn enough to meet some of these polished ministers. Why, some of them had been to college twelve years, and he had just finished high school. The first time

he talked to one he got so mixed up he didn't know whether he was a Mormon or what!

Then almost overnight he found himself. When he got the spirit of missionary work and really studied, so many things he had learned in the home ward came back to him that he found himself well able to defend and explain the Gospel.

All too soon his mission was over and he was home. Mother and father were still in the same old house with the same old stove. Every time they got ready to get a new one something like the ward chapel, the new stake house, or his mission had to come first.

The crowd at Sacrament meeting when he reported his mission was the largest he had ever faced. He felt just a little frightened when he stopped to think that after all many of these people knew more about the Gospel than he did. And then he saw his mother's face in the audience. She wasn't paying particular attention to the opening exercises. She was watching him. He had seen that same look of pride and joy before, but it seemed to stand out more than ever now.

Once he got started he thoroughly enjoyed himself. He had been rated one of the best speakers in his district and he would give these home friends the best that he had. And after all he was talking to just two people in the group. When he closed his talk with a strong testimony and sat down, he noticed that his mother's eyes were glistening with tears. He suddenly realized how much these people and this Church had meant in his life.

After the meeting so many people shook hands with him and congratulated him. Mother just put her arms around him and kissed him before the whole group. What a thrill it gave him!

As they walked homeward he put his arm around Mother on one side and Dad on the other. "Mother, do you remember telling me why you thought the five hundred dollars you put into the new chapel was a good investment? I know now why you thought so. May you never think otherwise."

687

The LOG OF A EUROPEAN TOUR

With President Grant and the Centennial Party

By LUCY GRANT CANNON
Of the General Presidency of the Y. W. M. I. A.

London News Agency Photo.
PRESIDENT GRANT ON THE BOAT TRAIN, WATERLOO STATION, LONDON, JUST BEFORE LEAVING FOR SOUTHAMPTON ON THE RETURN JOURNEY TO AMERICA.

CONCLUSION
Stockholm, Sweden.
Sunday, August 22, 1937

WE ENJOYED this morning's meeting with the Saints very much. The Church looked very attractive with its vases of flowers and curtained windows. Sister Larson says the sisters of the Branch have been scrubbing and cleaning for days to have it all as clean as it could be when we came.

The meeting tonight was well attended. The brethren estimated we had about 50% present who were not Church members. Father told us that very interesting experience he had when here about thirty-three years ago when he and his party called on King Oscar. It was the Fourth of July and in the morning he said to the party, "What would you like to do to celebrate our natal day?" No one seemed to have any special idea and so he said, "I know what I would like to do. I would like to call on King Oscar," and addressing his wife and daughters and the other lady he said, "Go put on your best clothes and we will call on the king."

King Oscar was at his palace on one of the little islands which comprise Stockholm. When the party arrived at the palace grounds, father suggested to them that they wait at a certain place and he would go up to the door and present a letter which he had written before leaving the hotel. If the letter were favorably

received, he would beckon with his hand for them to come to him. In the letter he had told that they were Americans, that he had a letter from the Governor of Utah vouching for him as a worthy citizen, and he enclosed the letter which the Governor had given him with the seal of the state of Utah on it. He reached the door, knocked, and

THE PRESIDENT AND HIS PARTY ON AUGUST 17, 1937, AT THE CASTLE NEAR COPENHAGEN MADE FAMOUS BY THE STORY OF HAMLET. LEFT TO RIGHT: JOSEPH J. CANNON, RAMONA W. CANNON, DANISH MISSION PRESIDENT ALMA L. PETERSEN, PRESIDENT HEBER J. GRANT, LUCY G. CANNON, JOSEPH ANDERSON, CLARISSA A. BEESLEY, PRESIDENT LYMAN.

handed his letter to the man who answered the door. In a few minutes another man appeared and asked in English what father wanted. Father replied, he wished to see the king, and the man replied that would be impossible, as those who saw him must be properly presented. Father said, "Did the king tell you to tell me that?" and the man replied, "No." "Well," said father, "I sent a letter to the king and I would like it back if he will not receive me. In the letter I have enclosed one from the Governor of the great state of Utah."

The man left him for a moment and in a few minutes he was told the king would receive him. So father beckoned to his party and they came up to the palace. King Oscar stepped out and spoke to them in Swedish. Then he asked how many of them spoke Swedish. Only three did. He then spoke to them in

faultless English. In the course of the conversation father told him who they were and about our missionary system. The king said many of the ministers of the churches in Sweden had asked that the Mormons be prohibited from proselyting in Sweden. King Oscar said he would not do this because he had sent his agents all over the United States to

ascertain how the Swedish people were faring in America, and that nowhere in any of the states did he find them so happy, contented, and prosperous as in the state of Utah. The interview lasted about ten minutes and was an experience to be remembered.

Monday, August 23, 1937

BROTHER LARSON had our trip planned so systematically he

CLARISSA A. BEESLEY AND LUCY GRANT CANNON ON THE STEPS OF THE L. D. S. COPENHAGEN CHAPEL.

TIVOLI, COPENHAGEN, AT NIGHT.

gave us a written schedule for each day. The one for today was:
8:30-9:30—Breakfast at hotel.
10-12—Missionary meeting at chapel.
12-1:30—Lunch at Grand Hotel.
2-4—Boat tour of Stockholm waterways.
4-6—Relaxation.
6-7—Dinner at Marnarita—City Hotel.
7:30—M. I. A. meeting.

We followed it as outlined except the breakfast was put forward half an hour so the meeting could be held earlier in order that we might visit the town hall before lunch. We were glad we did not miss a visit to the town hall. It is so artistically situated, overlooking one of the waterways. The most elaborate room was the banquet hall where eight hundred people can be seated. The walls of this room are in glass mosaic; millions of pieces of glass were used to make the mosaics.

After a fine Swedish luncheon we took a boat ride of about two hours, circling the islands. The sun was shining and most of the time a gentle breeze was blowing. Passing boats made waves in the water and we had the feeling of real sailing. Along the banks were hundreds and hundreds of pleasure boats of every type. Sister Larson says 40,000 people in Stockholm own boats.

In the evening we had an M. I. A. meeting and afterwards walked back to the tower where we could take our last look at Stockholm by night.

Wednesday, August 25, 1937

THERE were a few hours for us to spend in Gotberg before leaving for Oslo. We took the train a little after one o'clock. All the Elders and some of the Saints were there to see us off. There

was one dear old lady who came up to shake hands with father, and she said all her life she had wanted to see the President of the Church, but had not thought she would have the

SEEING STOCKHOLM THROUGH ITS WATER-WAYS. LEFT TO RIGHT: SWEDISH MISSION PRESIDENT GUSTIVE O. LARSON, PRESIDENT GRANT, SISTER VIRGINIA B. LARSON, AND PRESIDENT LYMAN.

opportunity now that she was getting so old. She said she had seen his picture often, but now to see

him was the happiest day of her life.

We said goodbye to President Gustive Larson in Gotberg. We had all formed a very favorable opinion of Sweden and her people.

As we neared Oslo we came in sight of the fjords and we were not disappointed as we viewed the Oslo Fjord. The calm water and the beautiful islands and hills make it a scene we will long remember.

At the station a large group of Saints and missionaries were there to greet us. President Peterson's young daughter, dressed in the colorful costume of the country, presented father with a basket of beautiful flowers from the Elders and Saints of Oslo. The Relief Society president also gave him a bouquet of roses from the Relief Society. We came immediately to our hotel and after about fifteen minutes we were off again to an M. I. A. meeting. Father rested in the hotel. We had a good meeting and a very fine group of people in attendance. We enjoyed the singing of the choir. My, how these Scandinavians can sing. We will all have to take off our hats to them.

Friday, August 27, 1937

YESTERDAY was one of the finest of the whole trip. Pres. A. Richard Peterson and family and three Elders went on an auto trip with us, taking us to see the fjords and the Norse museum and other places of interest. They called for us at about ten o'clock, and we took a drive out along the hillside, and every now and then we would come in full view of the fjord. It was a perfect day, with the sun shining (Continued on page 697)

A TYPICAL NORWEGIAN FJORD WITH ITS RUGGED LOVELINESS AND AWESOME BEAUTY.

Nineteenth Century L. D. S. Temple Architecture

THE TEMPLE AT MANTI, UTAH, (DEDICATED 1888).
UPPER: CELESTIAL ROOM; LOWER: STONE SPIRAL
STAIRWAY, LOOKING DOWN THREE STORIES.

ALBERTA TEMPLE, CARDSTON, CANADA, (DEDICATED 1923). UPPER: CELESTIAL ROOM; LOWER: BAPTISTRY.

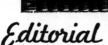

Editorial

To President Heber J. Grant, divinely chosen leader of the Church of Jesus Christ of Latter-day Saints, the staff and readers of "The Improvement Era" offer congratulations upon the eighty-first anniversary of his birth.

Forty Years

BEFORE me stand forty volumes of *The Improvement Era*—one for each year of its life. More than forty thousand pages, every one filled with entertaining, informative, character-building, faith-promoting material! How the *Era* must have blessed its readers from month to month! It forms a noble record of the works and ideals of a great people. As I turn the pages, thoughts crowd in upon me.

A book of remembrance was kept in the days of Father Adam. Ever since, men have recorded their thoughts and deeds in pyramid and palace, on polished stone or beaten metal, on papyrus, or paper, along the highways of earth. Upon the lessons of the past, thus preserved, the generations of men have built their own days.

Indeed, every generation should, in justice to itself and those who follow, leave memorials of its times. Thus, expenditures for permanent structures of use and beauty are justified. Statues, shrines, and temples, beautiful homes and notable business buildings, roads and bridges, pictures, music and books—all become parts of the book of remembrance passed on from one generation to help another. Every man's joy is in the sum of human possessions, to which his own contribution is necessarily small.

The Latter-day Saints have been faithful in recording their history. The Kirtland Temple, built at uncounted sacrifice, tells eloquently of the devoted faith of the founders of the Church. The Salt Lake Temple, rearing its six towers heavenward from the great American desert, reveals the unconquerable, certain vision of the high destiny of the Church. Farms, houses, cities, tabernacles, temples, and monuments cover the course of "Mormon" history. And this type of recording is continuing.

The story of the Church has also been told in written or printed words. The publication of a book, the Book of Mormon, is the most celebrated fact connected with the organization of the Church. Hundreds of other books, setting forth the claims and history of the restored Gospel have been authorized by the Church. Periodicals have constantly informed and inspired the people; these have now become invaluable records of bygone days.

The periodicals of the Church, past and present, form a most distinguished assemblage; the *Messenger and Advocate,* the *Morning and Evening Star,* the *Elders' Journal,* the *Times and Seasons,* the *Millennial Star,* the *Deseret News,* the *Journal of Discourses,* the *Contributor,* the *Young Woman's Journal,* the *Children's Friend,* the *Utah Genealogical and Historical Magazine,* the *Liahona,* the *Relief Society Magazine,* and many others.

In this illustrious company *The Improvement Era* finds itself. Soberly, on its fortieth anniversary, it surveys its history, duties, and opportunities. Humbly it looks back upon its own record of service; courageously it looks into a future of greater achievement. Gratefully it remembers the host of contributors and field workers who have made its success possible. It is doubly grateful for the men and women who as founders and editors have made it acceptable to the people: Presidents Wilford Woodruff, Lorenzo Snow, and Heber J. Grant, its founder and present editor, Brigham H. Roberts, Edward H. Anderson, Hugh J. Cannon, Harrison R. Merrill, and Elsie Talmage Brandley. It looks trustfully to the present staff, and knows that it will never want for capable help.

Today as before, *The Improvement Era* holds aloft its three-fold purpose: To record the current events and thoughts connected with the progressive life of the Church; to interpret events and opinions in the light of the principles of the restored Gospel, for the upbuilding of the faith of young and old; and to leave on the pages of the *Era* a truthful, helpful record of our own age.

Today, celebrating its fortieth anniversary, *The Improvement Era* voices heartfelt gratitude to all who have helped to make it successful, and it pledges its best efforts to serve the people of the Church in achieving their high purposes as Latter-day Saints.—*J. A. W.*

Woman's Changed World

THROUGH the pages of the *Era,* we have been emphasizing the tremendous changes which have occurred during the lifetime of our magazine. Strangely enough, the changes have revolutionized woman's sphere particularly. Where formerly woman's work kept her constantly bent over the tub or the stove, modern conveniences have emancipated her and brought a new, hitherto unheardof freedom. Hours of drudgery have dwindled into minutes of rapidly completed work. Where in years past woman was confined almost literally to the kitchen, today she has leisure to do much as she pleases.

What is woman doing with this new-found leisure? Therein lies the secret of her success or failure. Is she frittering away her time with senseless amusements or is she employing her time wisely to benefit herself, her family, her community, her Church?

The old saying about idle hands and mischief is as true—if not truer—than it ever was. With increased leisure, there is also increased mischief—and need for increased diligence in safeguarding our heritage.

From many sections of the country has come the information that most of our present-day trouble centers in young married women, who, having so much leisure, are using it to their destruction rather than to their salvation.

With the new leisure, many opportunities are afforded women to increase in power. Endless opportunities are open for mental and cultural growth through extension courses, study groups, and individual reading. With increased time, women could undertake a study of our civil institutions and with vigor clean up some of

(*Concluded on page 712*)

The Era's Three Decades as the Organ of the Priesthood

To the older men of the Church the story of the *Era's* many years as the organ of the Priesthood is perhaps familiar ground, but to the rising generation of young men and women it is one of those inherited facts which are accepted without historical knowledge. And so, in this fortieth anniversary issue we here review the steps through which the *Era* became a general Church-wide magazine.

In Volume XI, Number 1, November, 1907, pages 63 to 65, B. H. Roberts, speaking as a member of the First Council of the Seventy, wrote as follows:

Congratulations.—We congratulate the Seventies, first, upon their now having an Organ; by which we mean, of course, a publication devoted to their interests; to the development of their views; and the principles for which they stand; also a medium of announcement and publication of official acts. By means of the *Era* the First Council will be in constant communication with all the quorums of the Seventy in the Church. They will be able to suggest, advise, counsel, and direct the Seventies' work, both in administrative matters and in theological studies. . . . The *Era* has been the medium, of late years, through which nearly all important doctrinal and theological articles both of an official and semi-official character have been published, and it is these doctrinal papers that are of especial interest to the Seventies, since they deal with questions in which Seventies are, or should be, intensely interested; and are published in such form that they can be easily preserved and readily consulted. . . . And so we say to our Seventies, now that we have an organ, let us make use of it, both because it will give helpful suggestions in relation to conducting the special work of the quorums, and also because it will give helpful suggestions in relation to conducting the special work of the general character that will be helpful in preparing the members thereof for their labors in the ministry. . . .

The proposition has been equally welcomed by the Seventies wherever it has been presented to them, and is regarded as a most fortunate thing, both for the *Era* and the quorums of Seventy.

Seventies Era Agents.—The presidents of the respective quorums should at once take under advisement the appointment of an *Era* agent for the quorum, whose business it shall be to solicit subscriptions within the quorum for the magazine. . . .

The *Era* sends copies of each issue free to some two thousand missionaries in all parts of the world; it could not do this only that its agents who solicit and collect its subscriptions give their service gratuitously in the interest of missionary work; and it is on this basis that the First Council ask their brethren who shall be called to act as agents to accept the appointment cheerfully, and perform the work promptly and well.

Sixteen months later, Volume XII, Number 4, February, 1909, appeared this official notice on page 323:

Now that the quorums of the Priesthood are engaged in the formal study of theology, and meet weekly with this commendable object in view, there arises a need for a means of communication between the general officers who have the study and the direction of the quorums in hand, and the members and teachers of the quorums. This need, it has been decided by the Presidency of the Church, the Presiding Bishopric, the Committee on course of study for the Priesthood, and the General Board Y. M. M. I. A., will be supplied by *The Improvement Era* which from this date on becomes the organ of the Priesthood quorums and the Y. M. M. I. A. . . . Presidents of stakes, bishops and quorum officers and members are invited to take notice of this arrangement.

President Joseph F. Smith, writing in the editorial columns of Volume XIV, Number 12, October, 1911, noted the addition of the Church schools to the *Era's* broadening scope, when, on pages 1112 to 1113 he said among other things:

Already *The Improvement Era* is the organ of the Priesthood quorums, besides being the official organ of the Mutual Improvement Associations. At a recent meeting of the Church Board of Education, our magazine was made the official organ of the Church schools, both boards unanimously approving of this action. . . .

Attention is called to the statement of the special features to be presented in volume fifteen. It will be seen that many important subjects will be considered, and matters taken up that will be of vital interest to the general reader. We hope, as in the past, to make *The Improvement Era* the magazine of the home, in which both old and young members of the household will be interested, and in which the quorums, missions, organizations and educational institutions will be fully represented.

In all things, however, the spirit of the Gospel will continue to be the leading thread, holding all these institutions together, and the *Era* as in the past, will breathe the Spirit of our Lord Jesus Christ, seeking to present nothing but what is clean, pure, proper, and in harmony with his laws and commandments. This does not mean that modern thought and ideas which contribute to growth and progress will be neglected. We believe in progress, and that all truth is embraced in the great Gospel plan. We therefore seek these things, and will continue to present them in the light of the Gospel, and with a view to the furtherance of the great cause of the Lord—the Church of Jesus Christ of Latter-day Saints.

JOSEPH F. SMITH.

Subsequently, the Church Music Committee was added to the *Era's* widening scope, and in 1929, with the merger of this magazine and *The Young Woman's Journal*, the *Era* became also the organ of the Young Women's Mutual Improvement Association, at which time the First Presidency of the Church, writing in Volume XXXIII, Number 1, November, 1929, page 4, said:

It is not too much to expect that, combined with the *Young Woman's Journal* and with the aid of gifted women, *The Improvement Era* will reach a degree of perfection not heretofore attainable. . . . The *Era* will continue to be the organ of the Priesthood and the Church schools as it has been for some years past.

Offering, as it does, material suited to the tastes of young people, it has a well-defined mission to perform among them. The power of the destroyer is abroad. We read with bewildering frequency of appalling disasters on land and sea—floods, volcanoes, earthquakes, cyclones, wars and revolutions, and both ancient and modern prophecy indicates that in this respect conditions will not become better. Over these occurrences naturally no human agency can have control. But disturbances caused by the elements are not the only forms, nor indeed the most serious, taken by the destroyer. Concurrent with them and of far more consequence are the destructive inroads planned to wreck the character and faith of our youth. In this line of warfare the assaults are not made with storm and noise, but craftily. . . . The *Era* must continue to herald the startling truth that the Almighty has spoken, that man is created in His image, that the Priesthood has been restored, Christ's Church established and the plan of salvation made clear.

HEBER J. GRANT,
ANTHONY W. IVINS,
CHARLES W. NIBLEY,
The First Presidency.

Another step in a broadening Churchwide scope was taken in May, 1935, when the First Presidency announced Dr. John A. Widtsoe's appointment as editor, with President Grant, to assume active editorial direction of the magazine which now serves a worldwide Church.—*R. L. E.*

The Church Moves On

NEW TEMPLE SQUARE MISSION PRESIDENT APPOINTED

JOSEPH J. CANNON, recently returned from presiding over the British Mission and now acting as first assistant superintendent in the General Superintendency of the Y. M. M. I. A., was appointed by the First Presidency to serve as President of Temple Square Mission. Elder Joseph S. Peery who has served for the past five years in that capacity has been appointed manager of the Bureau of Information.

ST. GEORGE TEMPLE PRESIDENT NAMED—October 10, 1937

ELDER HAROLD S. SNOW, bishop of the St. George South Ward, has been appointed president of the St. George Temple by the First Presidency. President Snow succeeds George F. Whitehead, who has served as temple president since July, 1932.

President Heber J. Grant made the appointment at a special meeting of the St. George Stake Presidency and High Council.

Sunday, Sept. 5, 1937.

The Wasatch Stake was reorganized with Henry Clay Cummings as president.

Thursday, Sept. 23, 1937.

The headquarters of the Netherlands Mission have been moved from Rotterdam, Holland, to 292 Loan Van Poot, The Hague, Holland.

Sunday, Sept. 26, 1937.

The chapel of the Sixteenth Ward, Salt Lake Stake, was dedicated by President David O. McKay.

The New England Mission has been fully organized. The mission headquarters are at 7 Concord Ave., Boston, Mass.

SEMI-ANNUAL CONFERENCE

THE one hundred eighth Semi-annual General Conference of the Church convened in Salt Lake City, from Friday, October 1, to Sunday, October 3, inclusive. All Latter-day Saints were directed to adhere to the principles of the Church in every particular. In ringing statements, President Grant said:

I announced here at the Priesthood meeting last night and I decided to announce it again that we expect all the general Officers of the Church, each and every one of them, from this very day, to be absolute, full tithe-payers, to really and truly observe the Word of Wisdom; and we ask all of the officers of the Church and all members of the General Boards, and all stake and ward officers, if they are not living the Gospel and honestly and conscientiously paying their tithing, to kindly step aside, unless from this day they live up to these provisions. . . .

No man can teach the Word of Wisdom, by the Spirit of God, who does not live it. No man can proclaim this Gospel by the Spirit of the Living God unless that man is living his religion; and with this great understanding that we have before us now we must renew our loyalty to God, and I believe beyond a shadow of doubt that God inspires and blesses, and multiplies our substance when we are honest with Him.

The General Authorities of the Church stirred, the record-breaking audiences to a better understanding and an increased determination to follow the standards of the Church.

ORVAL W. ADAMS NEWLY ELECTED PRESIDENT AMERICAN BANKERS ASSOCIATION

ORVAL W. ADAMS, vice-president of the Church-controlled Utah State National Bank of Salt Lake City was elected president of the American Bankers Association at their 63rd Annual Convention, in Boston, October 13, 1937. Mr. Adams is a member of the Church Auditing Committee.

The nation's highest banking honor has come to Mr. Adams after a long and successful career as a bank executive and as a prominent participant in nationwide banking circles and activities. Two years ago Mr. Adams was made a vice-president of the same organization by popular acclaim from the floor of the convention, contrary to usual procedure.

MISSIONARIES LEAVING FOR THE FIELD FROM THE SALT LAKE MISSIONARY HOME ARRIVED SEPTEMBER 27—DEPARTED OCTOBER 14, 1937

Top row, left to right: Wilson W. Sorensen, T. Emerson Baggaley, Reid Richardson, Aldon Anderson, George A. Collins, Thomas E. Stolwarthy, Karl H. Hilbig, Arlo F. Johnson, Thorley Johnson, Lloyd L. Karren. Second row: John Van Limburg, Eldon Ricks, Melvyn A. Weenig, Don Orton, Don Jensen, Earl W. Smart, La Mar J. Wright, Ralph D. Kent, Garth S. Lunt, Sidney Priday, Calvin W. Wara. Third row: Grant W. Baker, John Dean, Keith E. Smith, Robert K. Cutler, Carson R. Healy, Russell Hochstrasser, Ivan L. Cluff, Albert L. Lewis, Gilbert A. McDougal, Ralph H. Jones. Fourth row: Verl Kartchner, J. Donald Earl, William G. Penrod, Karl Freeman, Lewis W. Smith, Elias W. Smith, J. B. Robinson, J. Ransom Hatch, Hyrum J. Amundsen, Jr., Duane S. Perkins, Arthur B. Nielsen. Fifth row: Gene H. Goosling, Wayne Bell, E. Enwood Thompson, Claude A. Burtenshaw, Rosslin Stringham, Anna Allphin, Clarence F. Tanner, Darrell S. Robins, Jason V. Nordgren, Paul F. Lindberg. Sixth row: Byron A. Howard, Fredrick G. Lisonbee, Eldon W. Cooley, Emmett L. Brown, LaVern Whetten, Winnifred McLaughlin, Annie Jarvis, Allan C. Woolley, Irwin Foster, Roy W. Spear, Herman Richards, Seventh row: LeRoy Clark, Richard G. Grismore, Hubert C. Lambert, Helen Moffett, Jennie Fonnesbeck, LeRoy Clark, Edna Smith, L. Flake Rogers, Eugene S. Hintze, Thomas Dyches. Eighth row: Aaron Jones, Dwight W. Smith, Lynn Buttle, Leona Cleverly, Emma Kendell, Dorothy Bowman, Alice Hanna, Dean Smith, Warren Stewart, Ralph Kendell. Ninth row: Howard R. Haggan, Preston D. Evans, Bessie Greenhalgh, Marguerite Christensen, Maurine Abbott, Elden Luke, Fern Dansie, Irene Elldredge, Delmer E. Simpson, Don R. Watkins. Tenth row: Max L. Larsen, O. Clement Williams, Calvin H. Bartholomew, Toynette Baird, Marjorie D. Collins, Mrs. LeRoy Clark, Carma Gamble, Paulina Black, Ken Wright, M. Floyd Clark, George R. Blake. Eleventh row: Max W. McKean, Louis J. Haws, Zella Scott, Donna Anderson, Selettie Morris, Ione Johnson, Dee Esta Burr, Lizzie D. Thomas, Darrill S. Bills, Wendell T. Jackson. Twelfth row: Claude Brown, Jr., Ferryle B. McOmber, Dean G. Griner, Barton Watson, J. W. Sessions, Don G. Christenson.

•What Church Leaders are Saying•

(Continued from page 660)

Los Angeles, California,
September 22, 1937.

"California hails the *Era* as the greatest mission-ary of the Church. In every home it enters it carries the Gospel message in a clear, interesting, and friendly manner. The *Era* is indispensable in the mission field.

(Signed)   W. Aird Macdonald,"
President of California Mission.

Lovell, Wyoming.

"Being members of an outlying stake we are especially appreciative of *The Improvement Era*. It is one of our best means of keeping in touch with the leadership of the Church. We feel it is a bond that unites us all together. Also, in our stake, *The Improvement Era* has been used very effectively in our missionary work.

(Signed)   Archie R. Boyack,"
President of Big Horn Stake.

Huntington Park, California,
September 25, 1937.

"The 40th Anniversary of *The Improvement Era* suggests three-fold felicitations: (1) Hearty con-gratulations to the *Era* itself; (2) Sincere congrat-ulations to President Grant upon his living to see his humble yet inspired efforts mature to the mag-nificent periodical now issued by the Church; and (3) congratulations to all the people of the Church upon the fact that President Grant still lives to bless them with his wisdom and leadership.

(Signed)   Leo J. Muir,"
President of Los Angeles Stake.

New York City,
September 26, 1937.

"The present day is one of excesses. The Church exercises wholesome restraints. Inquiries come daily as to what the Church is doing, as to its plans, its methods. Every person should have an intelligent answer. Give us the *Era!* It is a reliable source of information.

(Signed)   Frank Evans,"
President of Eastern States Mission.

Salt Lake City, Utah.

"I value *The Improvement Era*. I appreciate its vital messages on Church affairs and other live topics. Each month its pages are bristling with interest. It is a readable magazine and because of its fine ideals and standards it is a safe maga-zine for young and old to read.

(Signed)   Wilford A. Beesley,"
President of Salt Lake Stake.

LaGrande, Oregon,
September 23, 1937.

"Living as we do out in the world, we appre-ciate the *Era* as the instrument through which the voice of the Prophet of God speaks to us, and points the way to life everlasting.

(Signed)   Geo. Ariel Bean,"
President of Union Stake.

Ogden, Utah,
September, 1937.

"The modern test of the success of a magazine seems to require that it be instructive or entertain-ing, or both. Some periodicals cater exclusively to entertainment and others almost entirely to in-struction; but those of greatest circulation appeal to readers who are interested in instruction and entertainment.

"The *Era* has general appeal. Its instructive articles cover a wide range of topics of general information, and the Church matters give detailed and specific instruction that is almost indispensable to those who are active in Church work. Its stories and pictures are delightfully entertaining. And the gratifying thing about it all is that it is always wholesome and elevating. I have been a subscriber for many years and with the exception of few issues —which I hope some day to acquire—I have a complete file. As a reference work on Church history, biography of Church leaders and doctrine it is unexcelled.

"In fact, I think it is the finest publication of the Church, and I would not be without it. I read it from cover to cover. Those who haven't thus read it should do so and be happily surprised at the great wealth of stimulating entertainment and in-struction contained in it.

(Signed)   W. H. Reeder, Jr."
President of Mt. Ogden Stake.

Ogden, Utah,
September, 1937.

"A magazine one likes to read containing doc-trine, testimony and counsel. It promotes cultural development and stimulates higher ideals. A source of information on Priesthood activities, and the progress of the Church. I am grateful for *The Improvement Era*. Congratulations on forty successful years.

(Signed)   Samuel G. Dye,"
President of Ogden Stake.

St. George, Utah,
September 27, 1937.

"Congratulations on forty years of wonderful achievement and on the prospects of another forty years of continued improvement.

"*The Improvement Era* is entitled to the support of every home that wants the best in current literature. It is interesting, wholesome, vigorous, and inspirational.

(Signed)   W. O. Bentley,"
President of St. George Stake.

Phoenix, Arizona,
September 22, 1937.

"I do not know of an institution in the Church that is wielding a greater influence than *The Im-provement Era*. Its pages are filled with vital truths attractively written and illustrated.

"Congratulations on the marked improvement in the last few years in the publication. Maricopa Stake's goal is one thousand subscribers this year.

(Signed)   J. R. Price,"
President of Maricopa Stake.

Poetry

DRAMATIS PERSONAE
By Clarence Edwin Flynn

WE ALL are here—the hero and the
   clown,
The villain and the pauper and the slave
—To speak our lines, to win or lose a
   crown,
To move across the stage toward a grave.

We tread the stage, and strain our ears
   to hear
The clap of hands, or hisses rising high.
Where in the cast, oh friend, do you
   appear?
And which among the characters am I?

SO I MAY SEE
By Ora Haven Barlow

TRUTH is so great
   I often cannot see—

Like a blinding light
It shines before my eyes
And I see naught
And stumble in the path.

Help me to rise,
Great God,
This hour;
Help me to turn
This beam
Into the darkness.

Give me always
A portion of Thy power
To focus truth
In front of me
So I may see.

A GORGEOUS DAY
By Estelle Webb Thomas

YOU and I planned a gorgeous day,
   But it rained—do you remember?
And the wind blew chill and the clouds
   hung gray,
As they will in late November.

So we merely went for a walk instead,
While the gale rose high and higher,
Then home, with our cheeks and noses red
To read and dream by the fire.

But we found we had a gorgeous day,
Perhaps because of the weather,
For the glory, it seemed, was not in play
But in simply being together!

THE SINGING DUNES
By Lucia Cabot

(There is an old saying among the fishermen that
the wind in the grasses, and blowing through the
top sand, makes the dunes sing.)

THE WIND had played a melody
   Across the singing dunes,
And in my heart left echoes,
   The ghosts of little tunes.

And some were songs of happiness,
   And some throbbed deep with pain;
But silver songs from singing dunes,
   Are never sung in vain.

696

PRAYER OF THANKS
By Hilda James Worley

WE THANK Thee, gentle God, for love-
   liness
That through the seasons live on stem and
   tree,
For masterpieces on a changing sky,
The mirrored depths of every azure sea;
Then for the humbler, sweeter joys of home:
The ties that sanctify its every wall,
Our friends, our kin, and then a loved one's
   smile
To cast its gentle aura over all.
And last we thank Thee doubly for that
   hour—
The hour wherein our souls commune with
   Thee,
And in the beauty of that silence gain
Another step toward immortality.

LIGHTS ON A HILL
By Mildred Game

LIGHTS on a hill are stars swung low
   In answer to a prayer
To bless the houses in a row
And give them something rare.
Lifting the eyes of men that climb
In shining gratitude
That God has granted them the boon
To build a neighborhood.

QUEST FOR BEAUTY
By Anna H. Hayes

I SOUGHT thee, beauty, in the jeweled skies
   And warm, sweet breath of ocean-sighing
   wind.
I sought thee in the break of pounding
   surf
And where a rose-stream meadow quiet lies.

I sought thee in the distant market place
Where artist's skill has wrought old treas-
   ures rare
Of ivory and silver filigree
And silken strands of gold-encrusted lace.

I sought thee, beauty, in an arching dome,
In lofty spires, crested by the sun,
And yet, I found no lovelier sight than this,
Love serving life, within a quiet home!

TRUTH AND BEAUTY
By Nephi Jensen

BURSTING bud and blushing rose
   And glint of dancing star
Bring me Beauty's repose;
   I own all, near and far.

Serene Truth's regal reign
   My heart with faith empowers;
Peace holds my soul's domain;
   I own life's rarest dowers.

GOSSIPS
By Kathrya Kendall

THEIR chattering is like a clod
   Which—loosened from a mountain-
   side—
Bares grim destruction in its wake,
And oh, what lovely flowers hide!

CHOICE
By Margaret Coray

RATHER stars
   And shafts of candle-light
To flow across all hidden,
Grim, forbidden
Ugliness
Than burning white
Of day, that mars
All loveliness
By searching for its scars.

I HAVE A GIFT
By Aurelia Pyper

I HAVE a gift,
   But it's so very small
That some would say it is not
A gift at all.

It is not mine
To thrill the souls of men
By painting pictures, singing songs;
Nor yet again
Is given me
The power to uplift
With words of flame, yet I repeat,
I have a gift.

I cannot build
Great temples, it is true,
Or delve in mysteries of science,
But this I do:
I stand in awe
Before a canvas where
An artist shows he's searched his soul
And laid it bare;

I bow me down
On humbly bended knee
While someone speaks his words of faith;
In ecstasy,
I listen to
The songs the singers sing,
Or see the beauty and the joy
The others bring.

It isn't mine—
The power to create;
But still I have a gift, for I
Appreciate.

On the Book Rack

WHAT THEY WERE READING

November, 1897	November, 1917	November, 1937
Quo Vadis, Sienkiewicz, Little, Brown and Co.	The Dwelling Place of L i g h t, Churchill, Macmillan.	Northwest Passage, Roberts, Doubleday, Doran.
Hugh Wynne, Mitchell, Century Co.	Christine, Cholmondeley, Macmillan.	And So—Victoria, Wilkins, Macmillan.
The Choir Invisible, Allen, Macmillan.	Extricating Obadiah, Lincoln, Appleton.	The Citadel, Cronin, Little, Brown, and Co.
The Christian, Caine, Appleton Co.	Missing, Ward, Dodd, Mead.	The Seven Who Fled, Prokosch, Harper.
Captains Courageous, Kipling, Century Co.	The Major, Connor, Doran.	The Wind from the Mountains, Gulbranssen, Putnam.
In Kedar's Tents, Merriman, Dodd, Mead and Co.	The Salt of the Earth, Sedgwick, Watt.	

ON READING

"YES, SEEK ye out of the best books words of wisdom; seek learning, even by study and also by faith." These words, although spoken by the Prophet Joseph Smith in 1832, still have tremendous significance for us today.

The exhortation comes vigorously as a commandment that we must read not only good books but the best. As Latter-day Saints we are eager to keep abreast of the times. Our alertness to events is evidenced through our reading. It is easy for us to read if we make up our minds that we should read. We can find time to do the things which we want to do.

The difficulty arises in seeking out the best books. At the present time, in the United States alone, there are a little better than twenty-four books published daily. Imagine—a book for every hour of your waking and sleeping day!

Even if we had the inclination and the desire, physical limitations would make it impossible for most of us to read even one book a day, to say nothing of one book an hour. Our eyes would rebel at the strain; our minds refuse to absorb what was read; our bodies revolt at the restrained position.

We must therefore develop a discriminating taste and not be misled by attractive make-up and clever advertisers. We want health both mentally and spiritually from the books we read. We therefore need to choose as carefully the books we read as the food we eat. Many books have been tested by the acid test of time and have been found not wanting. In this class must come of necessity the Bible which, during all the years, has proved a consistent best seller. For Latter-day Saints must come next the standard Church works: the Book of Mormon, the Doctrine and Covenants, the Pearl of Great Price.

Senator Borah has developed a system which has proved worthwhile. For every new book he reads, he reads one that has become established. Books like Franklin's *Autobiography*, Cervantes' *Don Quixote*, Hugo's *Les Misérables* should be part of the common heritage of humanity. The more current, popular books should be read when their timeliness or their message warrants their being read. Link's *The Return To Religion*, Gulbranssen's *The Wind From the Mountains*, and Heiser's *An American Doctor's Odyssey* fall into this category. The passage of time will undoubtedly tend to decrease our interest in these books, but their timely message is worth our considering right now.

As we finish reading those books which we select, we should make a very definite criticism, including both the good and the bad points of each of them. We shall in this way increase our power to analyze books, and we shall become better readers and fulfill more nearly the commandment: "Seek learning, even by study."—*M. C. J.*

LOG OF A EUROPEAN TOUR

(Continued from page 689)

brightly, and just a few clouds in the sky.

We went to the museum which houses three old viking ships. One was unearthed in 1867, another in 1880, and the last one in 1904. These ships were in huge mounds, which when they were uncovered, were found to be burial grounds. The Osberg ship was found in 1903 and unearthed in 1904 under the guidance of the university. It is supposed to have been the burial ship of a queen who lived in the eighth century. When the ship was found it contained the skeletons of the queen, her handmaid, twelve horses, one ox, and four dogs.

From here we went to the Norse Folk Museum. We were especially interested in the room of Hendrik

Ibsen. It is reproduced just as he used it.

After visiting the museum we went for a lovely ride to a high point above the city where we had

a fine view of the city and the Oslo Fjord and the harbor.

After a hurried supper we all went to our rooms to rest for an hour before going to the chapel for meeting. Our meeting was a splendid one. When we arrived the people were all in their places and some were standing up. The congregation arose as father entered and remained standing until we had all come in. The choir made a fine appearance, all the ladies were dressed in white. The choir was a splendid one and sang with feeling and spirit. Father and Brother Lyman were the speakers and they had the attention of the audience all the time. After the meeting father remained to shake hands with those who were eager to meet him.

(Continued on page 708)

Homing

CONDUCTED BY MARBA C. JOSEPHSON

IT'S ALL IN A WOMAN'S LIFE

| 1897 | 1917 | 1937 |

This is the way we wash our clothes so early Monday morning.

This is the way we iron our clothes so early Tuesday morning.

This is the way we mend our clothes so early Wednesday morning.

The Improvement Era wishes to express its gratitude to the following companies for their courtesy in making this feature possible: Blackstone Washing Machine Company, Utah Power and Light Company, General Electric Supply Company, White Sewing Machine Company, Eureka Vacuum Company, Crane Company, Z. C. M. I., Ironrite Company, and the *Deseret News*.

1897   **1917**   **1937**

This is the way we bake our bread so early Thursday morning.

This is the way we sweep our floors so early Friday morning.

This is the way we take our baths so early Saturday evening.

This deluxe tub of the nineties was of copper-lined steel with a polished wood rim.

This is the way we go to church so early Sunday morning!

An actual reproduction of Z. C. M. I. advertisement appearing October 30. 1897.

Melchizedek Priesthood

CONDUCTED BY THE MELCHIZEDEK PRIESTHOOD COMMITTEE OF THE
COUNCIL OF THE TWELVE—EDITED BY JOSEPH FIELDING SMITH

COUNSEL AND COMMANDMENT

THE General Conference of the Church held during the first three days of October, 1937, was outstanding among the conferences of the Church in the outpouring of the Spirit of the Lord by way of counsel and commandment. The remark is sometimes made by thoughtless and unobserving persons that the spirit of revelation is not guiding the Latter-day Saints now as in former times. This thought can hardly be entertained by the members who crowded the Tabernacle during the three days of conference. To all who possess the spirit of discernment and the enlightenment of the Holy Spirit, it was very apparent that the Lord was pouring out His Spirit and giving to the members of the Church commandment and direction, which is most timely and needful in these days of increased disobedience and wickedness, which pervade the world.

Never, perhaps, has President Grant spoken with greater power and inspiration to the assembled multitudes of the Church than at this conference. Seldom have the members been called upon with greater power and inspiration to obey the counsels and commandments of the Lord; to walk in wisdom's paths and be faithful to principle and covenant, that the Church may escape the evils which are rapidly consuming the entire world. Never has there been a time when such instruction and commandments were more needed.

The world is rapidly being overcome by immoral practices. Men and women and even children of tender years are destroying their bodies with narcotics, stimulants, and other evil agencies; and these are finding their way among the people who are under covenant to observe and keep the laws of God. The standards set up in the Gospel for the Latter-day Saints are exceedingly high. They are based upon divine principles which have been revealed for the temporal as well as the spiritual salvation of the children of men. No other people in the world, as far as we know, hold such high ideals. We are taught that salvation hereafter, as well as now, depends upon keeping the body clean, sweet, and a fit tabernacle for the Spirit of God. How can the Spirit of the Lord dwell in unclean tabernacles? Paul cried out in words of warning to the Saints of former days: "Know ye not that ye are the temple of God, and that the

God destroy; for the temple of God is holy, which temple ye are."

One reason why the ideals and aspirations of the Latter-day Saints transcend the ideals and aspirations of other peoples is due to the fact that they believe in a literal sense that they are the offspring of God. He is in very deed our Father. We were created in His image and likeness, for it is written: "In the image of His own body, male and female, created He them, and blessed them and called their name Adam, in the day when they were created and became living souls in the land upon the footstool of God." The declaration of the risen Lord to Mary, is accepted in a literal sense. How else can it be received in reason? ". . . go to my brethren, and say unto them I ascend unto my Father, and your Father; and to my God, and your God."

What a glorious revelation it is to us to know that we are "begotten sons and daughters unto God;" that we are created in His divine image, even in the image of His own glorious body! What a sad thing it is that this great eternal truth has been lost to the world through their disobedience, and that Satan has gained such power among them, teaching them a debased doctrine in relation to their origin!

Since, then, we are the offspring of God, endowed with power through the saving truths of the everlasting Gospel and obedience to sacred covenants, to become like Him, and by the power of the resurrection—a gift from Jesus Christ our Elder Brother and the Only Begotten Son of God in the flesh—to rise to the great heights of eternal exaltation, how faithfully and jealously we should guard these bodies of flesh and bones! While they are now

corruptible and subject to the ills of mortal flesh, yet the promise is made unto us that they shall, through the resurrection, be quickened again and become eternal tabernacles for the spirits which inhabit them. If we have been faithful to every covenant and commandment, we shall then receive the reward of celestial glory. Our bodies shall be like the glorious body of our Redeemer, Jesus Christ, and we shall see Him as He is. "And every man that hath this hope in Him," said John, the beloved disciple, "purifieth himself, even as he (Christ) is pure."

With these glorious truths to govern us it is only natural for the Lord to speak through His chosen servants in admonition and commandment to the members of the Church, calling upon them to keep their bodies clean, their minds pure, their spirits contrite and their hearts broken.

It is hard to think that any member of the Church can fail to keep the Word of Wisdom, and have a desire to maintain his body pure and undefiled, if he understands the nature of the Gospel and the power of God unto exaltation. It is a mystery that so many who profess to know, fail in these holy and sacred things, for it is a sacred thing to keep the body undefiled and free from every power and influence which tends to impair and destroy its functions. If we do know the truth, and then refuse to abide in it, great shall be our condemnation. What excuse shall there be for the man who knows the will of God and does not heed it? The Jews claimed to be walking in the light of truth as it came down from Moses, but they rejected the Greater Light when he came to them with the fulness of the everlasting covenants of the Gospel. Jesus called them

(Concluded on page 707)

MONTHLY REPORT OF THE L. D. S. STAKE MISSIONS

*Made by The First Council of the Seventy to The Council of the Twelve Apostles
For the Month of August, 1937*

MISSIONARY ACTIVITIES

1. Evenings or part days spent in missionary work	4,514
2. Hours spent in missionary work	10,027
3. Number of calls made while tracting	8,130
4. Number of first invitations in while tracting	3,829
5. Number of revisits	2,563
6. Number of Gospel conversations	8,776
7. Number of standard Church works distributed	293
8. Number of other books distributed	318
9. Number of tracts and pamphlets distributed	13,664
10. Number of Books of Mormon sold	153
11. Number of hall meetings held	193
12. Number of cottage meetings held	427
13. Number of cottage and hall meetings attended	2,400
14. Number of investigators present at cottage and hall meetings	2,167
15. Number of baptisms as a result of missionary work	91

Aaronic Priesthood

CONDUCTED UNDER THE SUPERVISION OF THE PRESIDING BISHOPRIC—EDITED BY JOHN D. GILES

GRADING AARONIC PRIESTHOOD QUORUMS

For several years, a recommendation has been made by the Presiding Bishopric that, in wards where there are two or more quorums, a plan of grading according to age be followed. The recommendation is that where there are three quorums in a ward, the twelve-year-old boys constitute the first quorum, those thirteen years of age would comprise the second quorum, and those fourteen the third quorum. Under this plan, a boy would have a promotion on advancement from one quorum to another each year. This plan, it is believed, will increase interest and make it possible to hold more boys for the three-year period covering the Deacons' quorum activity.

In wards where there are two quorums, it is suggested that a division be made on the most practical basis, leaving the older boys in one quorum and the younger in the other. Where four, five, or six quorums are organized in one ward, the grading could be done along the same lines, keeping the boys of each age grouped together as far as possible.

An outstanding instance of the success of this plan is found in the Twentieth Ward, of the Ensign Stake, in Salt Lake City. The grading plan has been in effect for more than two years and has been very successful. Under the direction of D. J. Watts, Second Counselor in the bishopric assigned to Deacons' quorum supervision, three quorums have been organized, each with a supervisor, and each containing boys of the same age group. With the cooperation of Bishop C. Clarence Neslen and First Counselor, Louis R. Wells, this plan has now been standardized in the ward, with the result that there is increased attendance and activity.

LEADING STAKES IN QUORUM ATTENDANCE

The leading stakes in Aaronic Priesthood quorum meeting attendance for the month of August were the following:

	Per cent
Grant	62
Taylor	54
Star Valley	53
Maricopa	53
Juarez	52
Hollywood	52
Morgan	51
San Juan	48
San Francisco	48
Pasadena	46
Highland	46

The average attendance for the entire Church, for August, was slightly below the same month in 1936, but one point higher than for July. It is urged that Aaronic Priesthood supervisors devote special attention to the development of better quorum attendance during the winter months.

PRIMARY ASSOCIATION COOPERATION

Under the plan approved by the Presiding Bishopric, Aaronic Priesthood supervisors in all wards, in charge of Deacons' quorums, should cooperate in every possible way with Primary Association teachers of the Guide Class, which is composed of boys eleven years of age, and encourage all Primary boys to continue with that organization, until they graduate. At the time of graduation, the ceremony suggested for such occasions should be conducted at the Sacrament meeting, and all boys who have graduated and are properly prepared should be recommended for ordination to the Aaronic Priesthood.

For the past three years, the Primary Association reports indicate that there is an average of 85 per cent of all the eleven-year-old boys of the Church enrolled and active in the Primary Association. It is important that these boys be contacted by Deacons' quorum supervisors well in advance of their twelfth birthdays and urge them to qualify and prepare themselves to become Deacons. The Primary Association is in reality a recruiting agency for the Aaronic Priesthood, and every possible effort should be made by quorum supervisors to cooperate with Primary officers, in order that all boys may be properly prepared to receive the Aaronic Priesthood and be ordained at the proper time.

TINTIC STAKE VISITS CHURCH SHRINES

Aaronic Priesthood members from Tintic Stake visited Salt Lake City in a body on August 20, as the outstanding feature of the summer activity program.

Visits were made to President Brigham Young's Schoolhouse site, Eagle Gate, Beehive House, Lion House, former office of the Governor of Utah, Church Office Building, Deseret News, KSL Radio Studios, the State Capitol, Presiding Bishop's Office and other places.

At the Church Office Building, the boys were fortunate enough to meet Senator Reed Smoot, Postmaster I. A. Smoot of Salt Lake City, and a party of Senators and Congressmen from the East.

The visit was arranged through the cooperation of the Presiding Bishopric.

THE WORD OF WISDOM REVIEW

A Monthly Presentation of Pertinent Information Regarding the Lord's Law of Health

REPEAL AND "TEMPERANCE"

At the time prohibition repeal was being urged, statements were made indicating that real temperance would be promoted, drinking reduced, and bootlegging eliminated by the repeal of the Eighteenth Amendment. A statement issued recently by the National City Bank of New York City indicates that profits to the liquor interests in 1936, as compared with 1935, were nearly one-third higher. The profits for 1936 were $15,293,000, which is practically 18 per cent of the total investment. With the exception of three other industries: automobiles, automobile accessories, and drugs, the liquor profits were higher than those of any other industry in America.

HIGH SCHOOL GIRLS FROWN ON LIQUOR

An interesting survey, to learn the attitude of Catholic high school girls regarding the use of liquor by high school boys and girls, brought forth these comments:

"The high school boy who drinks intoxicating liquors is a 'show-off,' a smart aleck, vulgar, reckless."

"I do not associate with boys who drink intoxicating liquors."

"They're doing it to be smart or because they don't know any better."

As to their opinion of girls who drink, they were almost unanimous with:

"Cheap and common."

"Million times worse than the boys who drink."

"I think high school girls who drink are a decided menace."

"Unfit companions."

"Gives me the impression they are 'tough.'"

701

WARD TEACHER'S MESSAGE, DECEMBER, 1937

SQUARING OUR ACCOUNTS WITH THE LORD

THERE IS still left of the year 1937 enough time, for those who earnestly desire to do so, to square accounts with the Lord. There is still time in which to check back over the year and determine whether or not we have met our obligations in full.

The obligations to our Father in Heaven are of three kinds or classes: There are honor accounts, duty accounts, and financial accounts.

As Latter-day Saints, we have honor accounts. We have been taught the truths of the Gospel, the standards of the Church, and our obligations as members of the Church, and we have been given our free agency—placed upon our honor—either to obey the Gospel, or to violate its teachings. Unpaid honor accounts can be settled only by true repentance and a determination to make up for past failings by full observance in the future.

Duty accounts are those which place upon us the obligation to do the things required of us in our Church relationship. Every member has individual duties, family duties, and Church duties. A check of the past year will remind us of duty obligations which are unfulfilled. Here again only true repentance and a determination to make up in the coming years for remissness of the past can repay the obligations of duty.

Financial obligations include tithing, fast offerings, ward maintenance, and other contributions of money for Church purposes. At the end of the year is a suitable and appropriate time to check back and learn whether or not we have met our financial obligations to the Lord. There is still time in which to make amends for failure to meet these obligations.

As a New Year approaches, the best way to greet it with promises of success, happiness, and satisfaction, is to meet it with a clear conscience —with a knowledge of having met the obligations of the past year to the very best of our ability.

teaching the people by precept. How many who have accepted the Priesthood have given thought of the responsibility that comes with it? God has made His plans for our welfare; they are clear and comprehensive to those who have a desire to know His will and keep His commandments, there should therefore be no room for doubt in the mind of those who have entered the waters of baptism.

Some of us as of old are called to labor as teachers among the people.

To watch over the Church always, and be with and strengthen them; and see that there is no iniquity in the Church, neither hardness with each other, neither lying, backbiting, nor evil speaking; and see that the Church meet together often, and also see that all the members do their duty. (*Doctrine and Covenants*, 20:53-55.)

How many who hold the Priesthood are prepared and willing to carry out these instructions and how many must first set their own houses in order and be converted before they will carry out these instructions.

Every man holding the Priesthood should learn his duty, and to act in the office in which he is appointed, in all diligence. He that is slothful shall not be counted worthy to stand, and he that learns not his duty and shows himself not approved shall not be counted worthy to stand. (*Doctrine and Covenants*, 107:99-100.)

After careful study and prayerful preparation the thing most needed by an acting teacher is to be in possession of the Spirit of the Lord; if he has a desire to know the will of the Lord, his efforts will be blessed, and, if he is humble and prayerful, he will be guided.

He should upon entering the homes of the Saints, familiarize himself with the conditions of the home life. This can be done mainly through observation. It is not always wisdom to be too inquisitive or to ask pointed questions concerning home life, habits, and personal matters. Every visit should be characterized by gentleness, kindness, and the spirit of brotherly love. A teacher should never leave his home to make a visit without first asking the Lord for His blessings and the guidance of His spirit.

A teacher who believes in his work and who is in possession of the Spirit of the Lord is a welcome visitor in the homes of the Saints and the more often his visits the greater the happiness, the greater the encouragement, the greater the desire to serve God. We are strengthened through associating with the strong. We receive faith through works, and partake of the Spirit of the Lord when unity, love, and kindness have prepared us for its reception.

THE TEN LEADING STAKES IN WARD TEACHING FOR AUGUST, 1937

SIX STAKES reported 100 per cent of Ward Teaching in August, as compared with five stakes in July. Twelve stakes reported 90 per cent, or above. The ten leading stakes for August were:

	Per cent
Juarez	100
Los Angeles	100
Long Beach	100
Bear Lake	100
Oneida	100
Franklin	100
Weber	97
Big Horn	96
South Davis	96
Ogden	96

RESPONSIBILITIES OF THE WARD TEACHER

AND HE gave some, apostles; and some, prophets; and some, evangelists; and some, pastors and teachers;

For the perfecting of the Saints, for the work of the ministry, for the edifying of the body of Christ;

Till we all come in the unity of the faith, and of the knowledge of the Son of God, unto a perfect man, unto the measure of the stature of the fullness of Christ;

That we henceforth be no more children, tossed to and fro, and carried about

with every wind of doctrine, by the sleight of men, and cunning craftiness, whereby they lie in wait to deceive;

But speaking the truth in love, may grow up into Him in all things, which is the head, even Christ;

From whom the whole body fitly joined together and compacted by that which every joint supplieth, according to the effectual working in the measure of every part, maketh increase of the body unto the edifying of itself in love. (*Ephesians*, 4:11-16.)

To this end we are given the Priesthood and commissioned to go forth,

---

SHINING FAITH

By Ruby W. Simmerman

THERE are windows gold and shining, With God's light beaming through; There are clouds with silver linings, That bring us faith anew.

Sometimes we see the windows, But not the gleaming light; Sometimes we see the dark cloud, But not the lining bright.

Dear Lord: I thank Thee for the sun And all Thy glorious light; I thank Thee for the moonbeams— They make the clouds so bright.

I thank Thee for Thy care each day And for Thy wondrous love. Help me to understand Thy plan And reach to Thee above.

EXPLORING THE UNIVERSE

By FRANKLIN S. HARRIS, JR.

A NEWLY perfected tungsten incandescent lamp is coiled and recoiled to give 10 per cent more light, a light saving of ten million dollars a year. Usually the filaments are wound into a coil, but in this lamp the coil is wound 335 turns to the inch into very small coils, and then the coil itself is wound into another coil 70 times to the inch, and stretched between two lead-in wires instead of forming the present semi-circle.

✦

IF MAN'S voice were as powerful for his size as that of the tree frog, he could be heard from eastern Washington state to New York City, according to Science Service.

✦

TO eliminate the crackle and rustle of ordinary paper an almost noiseless paper has been developed for sound studios.

✦

INSTEAD of many strand barbed wire fences, animals can now be kept fenced with a single strand electric fence. Touching the strand gives a shock sufficient to discourage an animal from going through, yet will not injure it or humans.

✦

CENTRALIZATION of the fight on cancer will be possible with the three-quarters of a million dollar National Cancer Institute, appropriated by Congress.

✦

A puncture-proof inner tube is made by putting a layer of plastic self-sealing composition on the inside of the tube. A puncturing object can be removed and the holes will self-seal without loss of air.

✦

GLASS frying pans can now be used. A new variety of Pyrex type glass has been developed which resists heat so well that it can be used directly in contact with the flame.

WINDOW panels comparable to stained glass are afforded by a new translucent marble. Taking advantage of the crystalline make-up of marble, and by proper selecting and cutting, the interior structure of the marble can be shown. Ordinary light bulbs may be used for novel effects with fixtures or interior walls.

✦

ALFALFA has been found by South African biologists to make an excellent and palatable vegetable for human beings. Alfalfa gives good results in counteracting scurvy. It is unusually high in minerals.

✦

A DEVICE to be attached to a typewriter makes from one to four duplicate copies appear as originals, by using extra ribbons built into the machine. Another innovation is a white typewriter ribbon using aluminum for ink making possible typing clearly on blue prints or other dark colored paper.

◊ *Mutual Messages* ✦

General Offices Y. M. M. I. A.
50 NORTH MAIN STREET
SALT LAKE CITY, UTAH

General Offices Y. W. M. I. A.
SALT LAKE CITY, UTAH
33 BISHOP'S BUILDING

═◎═ *Executives*

Y. M. M. I. A. ANNOUNCES NEW FIELD SUPERVISION PLAN

WITH inauguration of the fall and winter season in the Y. M. M. I. A. a new plan of organization, motivation, and field supervision of the Scout, Explorer and M Men program has become effective. Under this plan a Church-wide program is to be conducted in cooperation with the Presiding Bishopric and the Sunday Schools which is designed to bring new vitality and interest in Church activity to every young man and boy in the Church.

The new Scout-Explorer plan includes some organization changes which place full responsibility for committee work as well as program promotion with Y. M. M. I. A. officers of stakes and wards. Aaronic Priesthood officers, who have in a number of stakes for several years cooperated in Scout and Explorer committee work, are now to be relieved of detailed responsibility in Scouting in order that their efforts may be devoted to Priesthood quorum supervision through the Aaronic Priesthood correlation plan, which includes groups representing Aaronic Priesthood, Sunday School, and Y. M. M. I. A. The full cooperation of Priesthood leaders is to be maintained.

The supervision plan for Scouting, which includes Explorers, is to include strengthening of contacts with National, Regional, and Local Council Scout Executives, frequent surveys of conditions affecting L. D. S. boys in Scouting, and active promotion of the wider use of the Scout program. The aim is to have every L. D. S. boy in Scouting.

A conference with Scout Executives in the central Church area, which has already been held, a survey of each council by the Scout Executive, and a survey of each stake through the stake superintendents were the first steps in the campaign.

More intensive supervision and additional field work among M Men organizations are also important parts of the new plan. More frequent contacts with district and stake M Men supervisors, plans for increasing interest in Master M Men activities and the use of the athletic program to build class attendance and activity are contemplated under the new plan.

M Men schools in each of the thirteen districts of the Church and a series

of special Scout-Explorer promotion meetings in various parts of the Church are now under way in accordance with the new plans.

John D. Giles has been designated as Field Supervisor for the Y. M. M. I. A. —with special assignments to the M Men, Explorer and Scout departments, and *Era* and Publicity.

John D. Giles enters the duties of this new position with a lifetime of qualifying experience behind him. In commercial fields he has distinguished himself in advertising, promotion, and selling activities. He has long been identified as an eminently well qualified "boys' man" in ward and stake

JOHN D. GILES, FIELD SUPERVISOR OF Y. M. M. I. A.

activities where for years he has done notable service in Scouting, Aaronic Priesthood, and M. I. A. work. In the Eighteenth Ward and Ensign Stake he has been a ward and stake superintendent of Y. M. M. I. A., ward Aaronic Priesthood leader, and stake high councilman.

He studied at the Brigham Young University, and after working in the business office of the *Deseret News* for five years established an advertising agency, the first in Salt Lake City. He was for fifteen years superintendent of the Y. M. M. I. A. in the Ensign Stake. He helped to establish the fathers' and sons' outings and the M Men movement. He has devoted the past twenty-four years to Boy Scout work and is chairman of the organization committee of the Salt Lake Boy Scout Council. He is executive secretary of the Utah Pioneer Trails and Landmarks Association and a member

of the executive board of the Oregon Trail Association. He has photographed scenes along nearly all of the Mormon Pioneer route from Nauvoo to Salt Lake City and gathered history for the erection of a large number of monuments erected along historic trails and sites connected with the history of the Church and the development of the western states. He is the author of a number of magazine articles relating to these subjects.

The new Field Supervisor came to the General Board of the Y. M. M. I. A. in 1929 and has earned much prestige in Church-wide circles as a "boys' man" since that time.

LET'S GO TO MUTUAL

THIS phrase has caught fire and is spreading all over the Church. People are saying it throughout Utah, Idaho, California, and the other states and missions of the United States and in England, Germany, Scandinavia, and in other foreign missions.

This is the way they say it in Denmark:

Lad os goa til Ungdomsmode.

And in Sweden:

Kom med oss till Utbildnings foreningen.

And in Norway:

La oss ga pa Ungdoms mote.

And this is the way they might say it in Germany:

Wir Gehen Nach G. F. V.

Let us use this phrase in salutation to each other as we meet in the home, on the street, at school, at business. The very saying of it will make us want to go to Mutual and when we get there the program is so delightful that we are sure to continue our attendance.

ARE YOUR COMMUNITY ACTIVITY COMMITTEES ORGANIZED?

A COMPLETELY organized community activity committee, with two energetic counselors as chairmen and well-qualified directors in the various activities as members, is one of the most important factors in insuring success in the M. I. A. program. Ward officers, if you have not already done so, make every effort to place on this committee directors in music and drama and dancing and in any other of the subjects you are taking up; especially the subjects being considered on the Assembly Programs. This committee has a fine piece of work outlined for this year and a real opportunity to enrich the lives of M. I. A. members. The reward in self-education and satisfaction in building up the entire organization will be great.

A HOBBY EXCHANGE

How would you like a Hobby Page in the *Era* each month?· A page where you could describe the thing that you are doing that gives you so much joy and cultural uplift and where you could read what other people are doing all over the Church? If you would enjoy such a page, indicate it by sending at once a brief, clear, snappy description of your especial hobby. Sign your name and tell where you live. We shall be governed in the publication by the number of responses, the character of the hobby, and the interest of the description.

DRAMA

All reports indicate the most general satisfaction with our 1937-38 Book of Plays that we have yet had. You will find a very interesting group of plays, from the simple comedies—which beginners can do—to big drama, calling for the best efforts of your most talented people. We are publishing this year individual copies of each of the eight plays contained in the volume. The ward must purchase at least one copy of the Book of Plays to entitle them to produce any one of the plays contained therein. Individual copies may then be obtained for members of the cast of the particular play being presented. Call your ward directors together and decide on some method of procedure in the exchange of plays by the wards, leading up to your stake Drama Festival.

DANCING

"There may be all the trappings of pleasure—rose color, gilt, tinsel, plush draperies, but despite all these, there is too frequently little spontaneity, little variety, no play, no mirth. The modern dance is essentially a dance for two and too often is not social. The two-some convention allows no opening out to sociability and friendliness. It is usually stiff, formal, and unimaginative." So says Maria Ward Lamkin, as a result of her careful survey of dance halls throughout the country.

Our M. I. A. is doing much to do away with some of the undesirable situations mentioned above, notably non-sociability, by introducing into our church parties group dancing and other means of developing friendliness and sociability.

We are also probably making history greater than we know by gathering something *definite* out of the chaos of modern dancing and giving uniformity of form, step and style to the Fox Trot and Waltz, by establishing "official" dances to be danced in every church dancing party. This will at least carry over to the oncoming generations some definite knowledge of the dances of this generation as we have knowledge of the dances of the past generation.

It is hoped that all directors have

begun to teach the M. I. A. dances, the "Aloha Oe" Fox Trot, the "Gleam" Waltz and the "Gold and Green Caprice." Your dancing parties will be much better by reason of it. *Let's have a hundred thousand dancing these dances by Christmas and make of it one of the greatest dance movements in the world.*

Axel A. Madsen and Emily C. Adams, Chairmen; Richard L. Evans, Dr. L. A. Stevenson, Grace C. Neslen, Laura P. Nicholson, Aurelia Bennion.

ENLISTMENT

Here it is November 1st and six weeks since the fall opening. By this time, every Adult member of the ward should be in the class or should be accounted for. If this is not the case, get a list of the adult membership from the ward clerk and visit each one. Mutual work has such a broad scope that there should be something to appeal to each person. Help each one to find it!

EVENING SOCIAL

Brother Oscar A. Kirkham tells of a friend of his who was visiting America, studying American life. What he considered typical of that life, he found one evening when he was invited to a home with a group. There he saw the group of friends gathered around the fireside, eating together, singing together, playing together, and talking together of principles rather than of personalities or things. When one is with a group of this kind, how can he help feeling the spirit of friendliness, cooperation, and growth.

Dr. L. L. Daines and Charlotte Stewart, Chairmen; H. R. Merrill, Dr. George H. Hansen, Lucy W. Smith, Hazel Brockbank, Vida F. Clawson, Polly R. Hardy.

Since the socialization of the Senior Group is our project, several of the wards have been thinking up ways to do it. One ward has used the Boy Scout plan for formulating "patrols" among the Seniors. These groups have come together on a common interest basis and are having some good times on the "patrol" basis.

Such a plan is effective where the Senior Group is too large to be well accommodated in a home. Of course, such wards will have larger parties in the amusement hall or elsewhere where the patrols may come together and thus socialize the entire class.

We shall be glad to hear of any plan that has really worked in the wards. Senior Leaders, will you not kindly have your scribe send in accounts of what you are doing? We'd like to know and pass on the good word to other groups.

BOOKS, BOOKS

We'd like to encourage much reading this winter. Of course, it would be well to start upon the reading course book, *The Return To Religion*, but while one member of the class is reading that book, if you are merely passing it around, another could read *Utah Sings*, or one of the other splendid books suggested in the Manual. A liberal education awaits those who will set aside some time for reading.

When you have read a book, report it to your stake leader and then we'd like the stake leader to report to us. We're going to give everybody who reads all of the books a right big credit mark. We'll call such readers successful travelers along the friendly road to an education.

Don't overlook the fact that *The Improvement Era* contains some rich material. The writer of these notes, as soon as the October number came, sat down and read the entire grist of poems. He was very well paid. Isn't "My Velvet Gown," by Zara Sabin, a delightful, old-fashioned ballad type of verse? Linnie Fisher Robinson's two little spots on the "Homing" page both have sweet memories in them.

All who have visited the Star Valley cheese factory and many others will enjoy "Star Valley and Swiss Cheese." In fact, the *Era* brings us many things of interest as well as importance. You will do a fine thing, perhaps, if you will take a few minutes for an exchange of "Eraettes."

M MEN

Frank W. McGhie, Chairman; Floyd G. Eyre, Dr. F. S. Harris, Homer C. Warner, Werner Kiepe, Dr. Wayne B. Hales.

More completely to inform all stake and ward officers and teachers associated with M Men of the many details of the varied programs of activities, the M Men committee of the General Board has scheduled institutes to be held in the thirteen M Men districts of the Church. Beginning on October 10, at Richfield, Utah, the entire committee accompanied by General Superintendent George Q. Morris, conducted the first of these institutes. The dates for the other districts are as follows:

October 17, District No. 3 at Ogden; District No. 10 at Los Angeles; October 24, District No. 12 at Phoenix; October 31, District No. 4 at Logan; November 7, District No. 6 at Provo; November 14, District No. 5 at Montpelier; November 21, District No. 8 at Twin Falls; District No. 13 at Cardston, Canada; November 28, District No. 2 at Cedar City; December 12, District No. 11 at San Francisco. Dates for District No. 7 at Pocatello and District No. 9 at Salt Lake City will be announced later.

Meetings will be held at 9:30·a. m.

(Continued on page 706)

(Continued from page 705)
and at 1:30 p. m. at which time complete discussions will be given on the following subjects:

(1) Organization, (2) Membership, (3) Joint M Men-Gleaner Activities, (4) Separate M Men Activities, (5) Manual and Teaching, (6) Athletics and the Care of the Athlete, (7) Finance of the M Men Program, (8) Cultural and Spiritual Activities, (9) Election of Officers for 1937-38.

Helen S. Williams, Chairman; Erma Roland, Ann M. Cannon, Rose W. Bennett, Katie C. Jensen.

TO GLEANER LEADERS:

THIS is to be your corner, where you may bring your questions pertaining to Gleaner work. Won't you write us telling of your hopes and plans, your accomplishments as this year goes forward?

Besides the 118 stakes in the Church there are missions all carrying forward this same great Y. W. M. I. A. work, and in writing to this corner, your questions, your answers, may help some far distant Gleaner group, so let us hear from you. Address your letters to The Gleaner Committee, c/o Y. W. M. I. A., 40 North Main.

Our first letter comes from Canada and reads:

The Gleaner Girls of Barnwell Ward, Lethbridge Stake, wish to send greetings to Gleaners everywhere. Though but a small group, we are very much interested in some of the highlights of vacation time. We hope other Gleaners have enjoyed the summer as we have.

Ever since school stopped in the spring we have held our Gleaner meetings nearly every week. We had not finished our lessons when Mutual stopped so we have continued them during our summer meetings, holding them at the home of one of our members who has been bedfast, and therefore would have been unable to get to any Church services at all, had we not held our class at her home.

Recently, having a little money in the treasury from our winter activities, we bought Gleaner pins, division sheets, covers, pedigree and picture charts, and postcards of Ruth the Gleaner for our "Treasures of Truth," about which we are very enthusiastic. We also surprised our sick member by a little token of our love.

The night that we gave her our present our lesson on Testimonies came. We hope that every Gleaner Class followed the suggestion given in the Manual for having a testimony meeting after the lesson, for that is what we did, and we all feel that we have never enjoyed anything so much. All came to the meeting fasting, and after the lesson had been given, each bore her testimony. Three ladies whom we had invited to attend our meeting, spoke to us first; and then each of the girls rose to her feet voluntarily and said a few words. There was a most wonderful spirit present. Girls who had never borne their testimonies before did so that night, and all felt that the Lord was indeed with us.

After testimony meeting a little social was held, each girl having contributed something to the light lunch that was served. Altogether it made a very outstanding evening that none of us will ever forget.

Barnwell Gleaners.

Dear Girls of Barnwell Ward—We were delighted to hear from you and now we find ourselves hoping that your same splendid planning will carry over into your winter's work. Are you all organized for the year with a Gleaner Girl president, vice president, secretary, and treasurer? There is such a big year ahead for your officers—the joint responsibility of conducting with the M Men on the first Tuesday of each month, the ten minutes at the beginning of each Tuesday night for your committee appointments, librarian reports on the reading course books, and the planning for your ward activities. Do let us hear from you again and tell us how everything is going up there in Canada. And we are wishing that every Gleaner officer who reads your letter will make time for testimony meetings and their Treasure of Truth books. Good luck and may you be blessed in your undertakings.

Gleaner Committee.

A Gleaner leader sends the following inquiry:

To the Gleaner Committee:
I am a Gleaner leader wondering what I am to do when I have only six girls, the only six in my ward. Our conditions are such that to carry out the entire Gleaner plan is impossible. Can you offer any solution? What shall we do? Just take part of it, and do it well or try to carry out everything as programmed?

A Ward Gleaner Teacher.

To Gleaner Teacher:
By all means, simplify the program to meet your needs. Draw from the suggestions given in the Manual those phases of the Gleaner plan which will help you most to reach the five objectives of Gleaner work, which, of course, you know are:
1. To know and live L. D. S. principles.
2. To establish normal social adjustments.
3. To develop ward and stake loyalty.
4. To train for leadership.
5. To prepare for eternal marriage.
Keep the spirit of wholesome fun and happiness alive in your Gleaner work above all. Success to you.

Gleaner Committee.

M Men-Gleaners

IT IS gratifying to the M Men-Gleaner Girl committee that so many enthusiastic reports are coming in, regarding the conjoint program. Working together, studying together, and planning conjointly is found to be the fun we anticipated. Co-education has proved itself to be the right type of education to develop the finer things that help to make life more enjoyable and complete. For the young men and the young women of the Church to develop their program on a partnership basis is in keeping with the kind of education that has developed where boys and girls work and play together. From the field have come the following reports:

The M Men in this stake have found out that we have to be on our toes, to keep up with the young ladies in our work,—the experience is interesting however and we are having lots of fun.

We didn't realize how much more interesting the class discussions could be with the young men present.

The young people of our M Men-Gleaner department are pairing off with each other as never before; we feel that the conjoint program has brought this about.

A little team work on the part of the M Men teacher and the Gleaner Girl instructor has been found to be conducive to an enthusiastic, interesting class. One report told of a particular ward where the young men's teacher and the young women's teacher take turns in giving the lesson. These two teachers have an understanding that each will do his best to enrich each other's lesson. When it is the Gleaner teacher's turn to give the lesson the Young Men's teacher also makes a thorough preparation and does all he can to add supplementary material. The young women do the same thing for the young men. That is what we call teamwork with a capital T! It would be difficult for a class discussion to lag with this kind of cooperation.

This fine spirit of cooperation is bound to carry over into the other parts of the program this winter. The banquet and the Gold and Green ball and other activities are all conjoint activities with responsibility equally divided.

Never before has there been such an enthusiastic response to the reading course books. Every Gleaner-M Men class should have a librarian who lends these two fine books to the class members so that all will have an opportunity to read them. The books are *How to Win Friends and Influence People*, by Dale Carnegie, and *Step A Little Higher*, by John Henry Evans.

SUGGESTIVE M MEN-GLEANER SUNDAY NIGHT CONJOINT PROGRAM

1—M Men-Gleaner Chorus.
2—Prayer, Gleaner Girl.
3—Solo, M Men or Gleaner.
4—Advantages of discussing "Youths' Opportunities with Youth."
   10 Minute Talk, M Men Leader.
5—"Why Should Gleaners and M Men Participate in Their Activities Together?" Gleaner Leader.
6—"The Living of the Master M Men Code, Makes Me a More Suitable Companion for a Gleaner Girl," by M Man.
7—"The Living of the Gleaner Sheaf Helps Me To Be Worthy of An M Man's Companionship," by a Gleaner Girl.
8—M Men and Gleaner Chorus.
9—Closing prayer, by an M Man.

Juniors

Marba C. Josephson, Chairman; Martha G. Smith, Emily H. Higgs, Catherine Folsom, Sarah R. Cannon.

CHICAGO STAKE offers this suggestion for our question box—an airplane, and airmail letters. And, may we add —answers to the letters, over station J. G.

And here are some airmail letters to you.

If you were having a dinner party, and some of your guests came when the meal was half over, handed you a bouquet of flowers, and said, "Sorry, but I have other things to do. Your meal looks delicious, but I must be running along," what would you think and how would you feel? What is your opinion of this kind of action at religious gatherings? May we suggest a campaign for this as a substitute. "Thanks so much for the opportunity. I shall be glad to sing for you some other time, but tonight I am singing in my own ward, and I would rather stay for the entire service."

How can Junior Girls live up to our department project, "We will show reverence for places of worship?" "Men are that they might have joy." But can you find anywhere a statement like this: "Thou shalt enjoy thyself regardless of any detriment it will do thine own character; of any annoyance it will cause thy neighbor; of any disrespect it will show to sacred places and things?" Or, "I am so glad I am early again tonight. I shall have a few moments to meditate in this sacred place before the crowd gathers. I wonder how the Lord felt when this building was dedicated to Him? I do hope we can keep the same sweet spirit always here that was present the day the church house was dedicated. Here comes the organist. Oh! hello, Mary Lou. Come sit by me and listen to this preliminary music. Is your mother better? That's fine. Isn't Mutual grand?"

We have launched, at different times, two slogans relative to the Sabbath and a weekly half-holiday; and we stand for spiritual growth through attendance at sacrament meetings. The sacrament meeting is the most important meeting in the Church for us women folk. What will you do for yourself and for others in your department to help us live up to this opportunity and responsibility?

Consider these letters. Decide which apply to your group. Help plan for progress. Do something about your plan. Rejoice in the results.

Continued, consistent effort will get us farther toward the star we have hitched our wagon to, than will spurts of enthusiasm.

Scouts

D. E. Hammond, Chairman; Philo T. Farnsworth, Arthur E. Peterson.

THE Boy Scout program is a valuable adjunct to the character-building influences offered in our Mutual Improvement Association work. Where leadership is ample and appropriate, fortunate indeed are the boys who belong. Where leadership is weak or vascillating, the program cannot be effective. Now that school has started and the M. I. A. is functioning at its best, some attention should be given to the improvement of troop leadership.

In most Scout councils leadership training courses are being offered. These should not be overlooked. A trained leader means better scouting and consequently better boys in the Church.

Many boys of Scout age are not yet being reached by scouting. This is the time of the year to initiate membership drives. The boys who have recently reached their twelfth birthdays, the dropped Scouts, and the boys who have never had the urge or desire to join scouting should be singled out, contacted, and urged to enroll. After these boys become members every effort should be made to hold them. If the leadership is efficient and the real scouting program is applied there need be little fear of losing a single member. In M. I. A. organizations where co-operation exists, reasonable effort made, and encouragement given, scouting usually succeeds.

Melchizedek Priesthood

(Concluded from page 700)

blind leaders of the blind, and said unto them:

"For judgment I am come into this world, that they which see not might see; and that they which see might be made blind."

"And some of the Pharisees which were with him heard these words, and said unto Him, Are we blind also?

"Jesus said unto them, If ye were blind ye should have no sin; but now ye say, We see; therefore your sin remaineth."

The members of the Church who heard the inspired words of President Heber J. Grant during the conference, and the members unto whom these words shall come, cannot henceforth rise up and say they have ignorantly sinned in relation to these great commandments. No officer of the Church, whether he is appointed to officiate in the callings of the Priesthood or the auxiliary organizations, from this day forth can rise up and make a valid excuse for disobeying the commandment to keep the Word of Wisdom, or fail

Two Brothers

(Concluded from page 683)

Pain was in both faces. A knowledge of that awful God-kinship between them! What similarity! What contrast! Compassion in one—despair in the other! Triumph and defeat! Salvation and damnation! Love and hate! Good and evil!

Together, wordless, they surveyed the jagged field. The pensive silence was eloquent.

The mockery of a smile bit like acid into Satan's somber, malevolent face. The Savior's clear eyes shadowed as he looked upon his brother, the outcast, the homeless one. He who had once been upon the holy mountain of God and had walked up and down in the midst of the stones of fire! And now he reigned alone in a world of his own creation, the angel of the Bottomless Pit!

An eerie glow like dawn shone forth from the whiteness of Christ. A soft radiance fell, and, in the light, the face of Lucifer looked old and infinitely tired.

Something intangible was in the air. An emotion beyond the comprehension of man hovered there. It was as though each strove to reach over the abyss of time. To realize again the harmony of their creation. Memory cried out like a weird strain from some unearthly, ethereal place. And then as it had come like strange music, so it left.

The screaming again. The flashing! The flaming! I was sinking . . . sinking . . . and then I pressed my eyes tight shut to keep out the millions of fire-specks dancing there.

Wings thrummed. Deep, resounding roars shook the earth. Cool fingers of rain stroked my face. I opened my eyes.

They were gone! And the battlefield was left to struggling humanity and to the wind which sighed and moaned like a woman over the blood, the bones, and the broken flesh.

---

to observe the Sabbath day and keep it holy, or refuse to pay his honest tithes and offerings.

It is the duty of the men who are called to preside in the quorums of the Priesthood to see that these admonitions and commandments are laid before the members of the quorums, and that they are properly and sufficiently taught. Every person in the Church who loves the truth and desires to obey its precepts, will rejoice and turn to the Lord with renewed faith and keep every covenant and commandment.

—*J. F. S.*

Log of a European Tour

(*Continued from page 697*)

August 29, 1937

We left our hotel yesterday morning soon after eight and were at the station for some time waiting for the train. We were not able to reserve seats on the train so we went early to get good seats. We were not in compartments this time. The cars are narrower than ours at home; the aisle is at the side of the seat for two, and then on the other side is a single seat. We occupied the double seats and three men the single ones. Opposite us was a nice looking Japanese gentleman.

We went up 4,000 feet to reach the summit and were above the timber line. Here the vegetation was very scarce and the rocky tops of the mountains bare of green. We came quite close to a glacier, and it reminded us of the glaciers in Alaska. We could see the deep blue coloring. As we came down we rode into very high mountains, and for many miles along the banks of a large fjord. It was a most magnificent view to see the towering, thickly wooded mountains extending down into the water. The water was so clear it acted as a mirror and the mountains looked as if they went down into the water.

When we arrived at Bergen there was a goodly group of people, missionaries and Saints, who welcomed us. The city nestles right down at the side of a high mountain.

The meeting tonight was a splendid one. The house was crowded

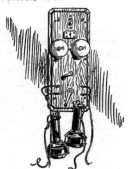

OLD TYPE TELEPHONE-MAGNETO WALL SET—A FAMILIAR OBJECT OF THE NINETEENTH CENTURY. (FOR THE MODERN VERSION SEE PAGE 726.)

and many people stood during the entire service. As in Oslo, all the ladies of the choir were dressed in white.

Father spoke for a little over an hour and we were all delighted with his sermon. He seemed to speak with great ease and the interpreter did well, so the brethren who understood told us. We have held tonight the last scheduled public meeting. Twenty-four days have passed since we left London for the Scandinavias and tonight as we reflect on the activities of these three weeks we are filled with satisfaction. Our meetings have been well attended, the newspapers have published friendly material, the

people have extended every courtesy and given us every consideration. The scenery and weather have united in making their contributions of beauty and so we all feel happy over this trip and are assured that the Church will profit by father's visit.

Tuesday, August 31, 1937

YESTERDAY morning Saints and Elders were at the docks to see us off. The weather was ideal, all the clouds and mists of the day having cleared away and all was propitious for a pleasant voyage. As we were standing on the ship *Venus*, waiting for it to pull out, someone suggested that father sing "O Ye Mountains High." He sang all the verses, and we on the ship and the missionaries and a few of the Saints standing on the shore, joined in the last part of each stanza. Then all sang the chorus of "Carry On," we on the ship singing in English and those on the shore singing in Norwegian. As the ship began to move away the strains of "We Thank Thee, O God, For a Prophet," came up from the group on the shore. There was a calling of goodbye, handkerchief waving, and the ship turned slowly, and we were out of sight of those people who had welcomed us so heartily and done all in their power to show their appreciation of father's visit.

Today has been spent on the train. We arrived at Newcastle, England; about 8 a. m. and were there about an hour and a half before we left the boat. We had to show our passports a few times, have our baggage inspected, and then were at liberty to take the train.

London, Wednesday, September 1, 1937

TONIGHT we had an M. I. A. meeting with the mission board and the Elders who were interested in the work. There has been some very good M. I. A. work done here in this mission and we were happy over the bright outlook for the work this winter.

Thursday, September 2, 1937

TODAY we have been shopping again, and visiting some places of interest. The whole party ate lunch at Cheshire Cheese Inn. This is a famous inn where Dickens, Johnson, Boswell, and many other notables came to eat and drink their glasses of beer. This building was rebuilt in 1669 and has been practically the same since then. We were shown the seats where Dickens and Johnson always sat. There is a copy of Johnson's first diction-

The Advertisers

When **The Improvement Era** started upon its career forty years ago, under the capable and aggressive business management of Heber J. Grant, more than a score of loyal and enterprising national a n d western institutions gave their support through the advertising columns of the first volume.. Of those whose names appeared in the **Era** then, several have survived the two-score years of change and are represented in this Fortieth Anniversary Issue, among them—

To the advertisers of forty years ago, and to all the progressive and fore-sighted institutions that have come into our pages since that time, the editorial and business management of **The Improvement Era** extends appreciation for the **Era** and for its great host of Churchwide readers.

Log of a European Tour

ary. It consists of two volumes, each one as large as our dictionary, some first editions of Dickens' works, pictures, chinaware, and other relics of the past. The management tries to keep up the tavern just as it was three hundred years ago. They use willowware china on quaint old salt and pepper shakers and serve their famous beef and kidney pie on plates of the same pattern.

After leaving Cheshire Cheese Inn we visited the home of Samuel Johnson. This house has been a museum for about forty years. The guide, a delightful lady and an ardent admirer of Johnson, gave us a feeling for Johnson that we never had before. His family life and his great humanitarian qualities were emphasized. She told us of his caring for hundreds of poor people and for thirty years keeping in his home a blind woman who was no relation and who was so disagreeable that he often had to bribe the maids to stay and care for her.

We went from room to room where furniture and pictures and bric-a-brac were just as it was in his day. We were taken into the attic where he did his writing and where his wife never came to disturb him.

Friday, September 3, 1937

WE are all quite excited tonight and have been humming "And It's Home Again, Home Again, America For Me," several times today. Our last day in London has been spent by father in visiting newspaper men and steamship company officers, counseling with Brother Lyman, writing in books for the Elders, a visit to the Kew Gardens, the most famous of all botanical gardens in the world, and lastly being entertained by Brother and Sister Lyman. Sister Beesley and I, guided by Sister Ramona Cannon, visited two art galleries, the Tate and Wallace; walked around the Parliament buildings and out over the Thames River. We looked longingly at Westminster Abbey. Our one disappointment was not being able to go into the Abbey. It has been closed to the public ever since the Coronation of King George, so we are among those hundreds of thousands who have been on the outside.

Tonight we rode around on the upper deck of a bus, looking and looking for the last time. We stopped at Trafalgar Square, Piccadilly,
(Continued on page 710)

Log of a European Tour

(Continued from page 709)

rode down the Mall, and walked over the Thames again.

Saturday, September 4, 1937

WE were all up early this morning and ready long before time to go to the station. Brother Lyman called at the hotel for us and when we reached the station President and Sister Clark, President and Sister Lyman, many of the missionaries and some of the Saints were there to say goodbye. There was the usual snapping of cameras, messages to loved ones at home, and finally as the time for the train to pull out arrived, the Elders and Saints gathered in a group and sang "God Be With You Till We Meet Again." Just as the train was pulling out they all sang "We Thank Thee, O God, For a Prophet."

Brother Lyman went with us as far as Southampton, where we boarded the boat, *The Empress of Britain.* Mr. J. A. Martin, the manager of the Canadian Steamship Company, came on the boat to wish father goodbye, and suggested that anything that could be done for his pleasure or convenience would be done. Brother Lyman was invited to stay to lunch and was the guest of the Steamship Company. Brother Lyman suggested to the waiter that he call him in plenty of time so that he could leave the ship, which he said he would do. At five minutes after one we began to notice the boat moving a little, and upon getting up we discovered that we were drawing away from the shore. The waiter had miscalculated the time and so Brother Lyman was still on board. Arrangements were made with the ship's officers to have the tug come up alongside of the vessel and take Brother Lyman ashore. In about twenty minutes the tug came up alongside of the ship, the gangplank was dropped and Brother Lyman stepped on to the tug. We called goodbye and we all waved our handkerchiefs, he doing the same from the tug. We watched until his boat turned into the harbor.

Wednesday, September 8, 1937

THE voyage thus far has not been very rough, but father and I have both thought it the better part of wisdom to remain in our cabins. We are looking forward to landing tomorrow, and then our tour will be practically completed. Sister Beesley goes to Chicago, Sister Bennett and Sister Wallace to New York, father and Brother Anderson to Salt Lake, and I to Toronto.

(Concluded on page 712)

For many years before and after the turn of the century, this Bank occupied the building shown below, just across Main Street from its present 16-story building, its home since 1912.

P R O G R E S S

Growth of this intermountain institution is typified not merely in terms of stone and steel and bricks . . . but also in scope of services, in strength of resources and in the experience of successful management. These are benefits offered to the customers of this Bank. Your account is cordially invited.

WALKER BANK
& TRUST COMPANY

Salt Lake City

MEMBER FEDERAL DEPOSIT INSURANCE CORPORATION

Log of a European Tour

(Concluded from page 710)

I have purposely avoided mentioning many names, because so many have helped to make our visit pleasant, that had I mentioned all, this log would have been but a chronicle of names.

However, I can not close without expressing our deep appreciation to President Lyman who for two months guided our party, looked up railroad schedules, prepared maps, and wrote letters to the mission presidents, giving the time of arrival, the time of departure, the number of meetings to be held, saw that every minute of the time was used to advantage but that father was protected as much as possible. He said he wanted father to leave the mission better in every way than when he came; he wanted this trip to be a vacation as well as a missionary journey. And so each day had its rest periods as well as its meetings. We are all agreed, father included, that Brother Lyman did his work well because, notwithstanding it was a strenuous trip with many changes of trains, hotels, and diet, father is coming home in as good health, if not better, than when he left; and had it not been for Brother Lyman's generalship, father might have returned quite worn out. As it is, it has been so pleasant, father is already talking of a return trip some two or three years hence.

And so, as an author reluctantly lays down his pen when he has written "The End" to a loved book, I will close by again expressing my appreciation for this rare opportunity of accompanying my beloved father on this memorable journey.

Woman's Changed World

(Concluded from page 692)

our vicious political practices. With the new leisure, our spiritual growth should transcend all previous development, for with this new leisure mothers have time to instruct their children better in the rightness and wrongness of certain behavior.

Women have always been rightly considered the guardians of the best in civilization. Unless they regard this new leisure as an opportunity for an increasing of the best and a diminishing of the worst which the age offers, we shall find that this free time will serve as a prelude to the downfall of our generation. If, however, women accept the new leisure as a responsibility for greater development, then they will become active factors in the realization of the millennium to which we are eagerly looking.—*M. C. J.*

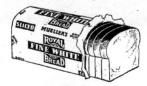

Watch for the "Era's" New Continued Story.

Patronize These Advertisers and Mention the "Era."

THE OUTLAW OF NAVAJO MOUNTAIN

(Continued from page 677)

freshments on the fire, and when those refreshments had only begun to sizzle, a greater posse joined Oliver and came through the gate.

Posey's people might stop somewhere later on, but not right there; they must be moving. Some of them, ravenous with hunger, gulped part of their half-cooked victuals with swine-like dispatch, but they threw the rest away and piled the loads back on their horses in a jumble.

To hold their course now to Recapture meant to meet the posse in the open flat. That simply couldn't be—it was contrary to the very first principles of their warfare. They would have to go back, for the whistle of bullets admonished them that the posse had guns as big as their own.

"What about my brother?" whined the second wife, "What can we ever do without him?" and she hesitated as if she would go on to Recapture at all hazards.

"To h— with your brother!" roared the distracted Posey. "It's easier for him to come to us than for all of us to go to him."

It was not possible for them to know it that day, and certain ones of them were to die before it could be reported that Poke listened with nothing but disgust to Posey's messenger and then grunted, "Puneeh! He learns no more than a skunk, and they will kill him for making such a big stink."

And then the old grizzly packed up and moved farther over into Colorado, camping near a ranch in McElmo where he could hear from the fight without being near enough to be blamed or praised for the nature of its outcome.

Three squaws and two papooses were so sure that Poke was their only hope of deliverance, that they dropped out of the company on Murphy Point and were later found hiding in a cave half way to Yellow Jacket.

Posey and his company, keeping out of sight behind the cabin, hurried west for the nearest rocks. And there in the rim of White-Mesa Canyon their main

snipers hid while their company rode lash and lather down through the rocks to cross to the west side.

His people descended into the canyon on the lope, treading each other's heels and jostling violently at every turn of the trail, while Posey lay, watching the little notch in the rim from which they came off the point, resolved to bore the first man who appeared behind them.

At that first man, who happened to be John D. Rogers, he let fly with his big gun, expecting to cut his man through the lungs from the side. But the shot went low, it barely grazed John's hip pocket, pierced the tree of the saddle and broke the back of the horse.

When the general saw the horse drop, the rider leap from sight and no one else appear, he craned his neck to scan that vicinity, and incidentally to look behind and to one side. Then he discovered in the distance a car coming from town to head his people from crossing the road on the west side of the canyon.

(Continued on page 718)

Next Month George D. Pyper Continues "The Story of Our Hymns."

ANNUALLY, thousands of baseball fans throughout the nation await "world series" time. For then the year's most closely followed sports broadcast is brought them through the Columbia Broadcasting System. For many seasons, now, KSL has served downtown s p o r t s followers exclusively through cooperation with the Tribune-Telegram.

This year once more it was KSL exclusively that installed the giant public address system informing a visual audience of thousands as play progressed in the Yankee Stadium and in the Polo Grounds.

The KSL photographer "caught" a portion of the listening and watching crowd during one of the games this fall. KSL's huge speakers are shown in the circle, addressing a traffic-stopping crowd that, on Salt Lake's Main street heard the crack of bat on ball, the cries of players and fans as the Yankees drove to their world championship.

KSL continues to look for new outlets, new means of serving the vast Intermountain and Western audience that depends on "The Voice of the West" for entertainment, for news, for public events coverage.

KSL — AFFILIATED WITH CBS — 50,000 WATTS — THE VOICE OF THE WEST

SOLUTION TO OCTOBER PUZZLE

	F	A	I	T	H		G	U	I	D	E	
H		S	M	E	E	S		T	R	U	T	H
O	M		P	E	A	C	E		A	S	H	Y
P	A	L		S	T	R	A	P		T	E	
E	N	O	S		H	A	G	A	R		R	I
	N	O		D	E	M	E	T	E	R		D
J	A	S	P	E	R		R	E	F	U	G	E
O		E	O	N		C		N	E	B	O	
Y		T	S	A	R	S		R	E	A	R	
	E	L		E	G	O		H		S	T	E
A	N	O	N		O	W	N	E	R		S	S
R	I	V	E	N		N	O	R	I	A		T
	M	E	R	C	Y		G	R	A	C	E	

NO. 52

SCRIPTURAL CROSSWORD PUZZLE
Crowning the King (II Kings 11:12)

© W. A. W. Co.   NO. 10

ACROSS

1 "when . . . had called to the king"
2 "Because thou hast . . . thine hands"
10 "We . . . all like bears"
11 One of the "shipmen" with Paul when the ship was wrecked
12 Allure
14 Raise
16 "the people fled into . . . tents"
17 "clean . . . , and a pure heart"
18 Note
19 "thou hast . . . me out this day"
21 The month that comes in ten years
23 Unit of energy
25 Enterprise
27 ". . . forty years reigned he in Jerusalem"
29 "And he . . . , To thee, O captain"
30 "both his . . . shall tingle"
32 "he reigned . . . year in Jerusalem"

34 Mandan is in this state, and the state is in Mandan
35 Long narrow inlet
36 "neither after him arose there . . . like him"
38 "and for the . . . that is in the land of Assyria"
39 "O Lord our . . . , I beseech thee"
41 "come up, and . . . me out of the hand of the king of Syria"
43 Bark of E. Indian tree; a pine (anag.)
45 Bodies of partisans
47 New England state
48 A chill
49 Born
50 "they brought . . . king word again"
51 "and made a . . . over themselves"

Our Text from Kings is 1, 4, 16, 17, 27, 29, 39, 41, 50, and 51 combined

DOWN

1 Threaten a fall; thrones do this
2 "The king of Moab . . . rebelled against me"
3 "have . . . concerning the faith"
4 Animal held in high esteem in Egypt, but not mentioned in the Bible
5 Chinese weight; beginning of life
6 Independent state in Europe
7 East Indian tree
8 Incited
9 Speck
10 Sun god
11 Light fabric
13 Displayed
15 Compass point
17 Battle formation; sheer (anag.)
18 "and to be had in . . . of all them that are about him"
20 National officer
22 Boiled down; second end (anag.)

24 Car house
26 This chapter of Second Kings tells about the Syrian army being smitten with blindness
28 Canadian province
31 City east of Bethel; animal
32 City in Egypt; preposition
33 Empire State
34 Six states
36 "The fear of the Lord is the beginning of wisdom" is one
37 "thou shalt not call her name . . . , but Sarah shall her name be"
38 "Jehoshaphat . . . the king of Judah"
40 Large fish
41 Continent
42 New England state
44 "And so . . . came to pass"
45 Hebrew letter in Psalm 119
46 Early English

The L. D. S. Business College Spans Half a Century of Progress

—and the faculty of today maintain the ideals set by the founders of the school.

Milton H. Ross
Penmanship Bookkeeping

Heber C. Kimball
Accounting

Iris Irons
Typewriting

Edna B. Clawson
Typewriting

Joyce Richardson
Bookkeeping

Vernon F. Larsen
Ethics

Mabel Brown
Shorthand

Allien Russon
Shorthand

Gweneth G. Gates
Secretary

E. Claud Jenson
Office Machines

FERAMORZ Y. FOX, President

Believing that the strength of the institution is its faculty, the L. D. S. Business College has selected a staff of workers who are not only experts in their respective fields, but who are particularly well qualified to promote the welfare of young men and women.

It is the pledge of this school that every student shall have the greatest possible opportunity to qualify for business employment.

Information about courses, methods of instruction, employment service, etc., will be gladly furnished.

●

Day and Evening Classes
All the Year

Eugene C. Hinckley
Shorthand

Elsie Kienitz
Treasurer

Florence P. Evans
Shorthand

Lillian R. Smith
Office Training

Miriam Parker
Office

Le Ray S. Howells
Accounting

Maud N. Leaver
Employment

Katie C. Jensen
Personal Development

Walter E. Elieson
Law, Salesmanship

Norma Knight
Stenotypy

Kenneth S. Bennion
English

Helen Shurtleff
Office

L. D. S. BUSINESS COLLEGE
(A Department of the L. D. S. College)

70 North Main Street   Salt Lake City, Utah   Wasatch 1812

THE OUTLAW OF NAVAJO MOUNTAIN

(Continued from page 714)

He crept around hurriedly to a position from which he could rake the seats of that T Model as it passed, waiting eagerly while it sped nearer. Three men occupied the back seat, two in front. Two cartridges should finish the five of them.

In spite of his bead on the coveted prize, his first shot pierced the car just behind the men in the back seat. Four inches ahead it would have gone through the lungs of Warren Allan, George Hurst, and Frank Redd.

Of course Posey knew nothing of how near or how far he had missed, but he did know that little car rattled right on and would be out of range in a very few seconds, so he aimed for a wheel and punctured a tire. The machine wabbled and stopped in an open space where no rocks or banks could hide his prey from him. They were his!

The five men in that car would have been his game right away, but John D. Rogers and Leland Redd saw the smoke from his sniper's nest and made life so perilous in that vicinity that he got out in a hurry and rushed on to join his people before he was cut off from them.

Late on that March afternoon the galloping fugitives approached Ruin Spring, nine miles southwest of Blanding, and appropriated six horses grazing in a field. This represented all the plunder of the big stir this far.

With their children sniveling for supper and their goats panting and ready to go on strike at this racehorse style of travel, they entered the narrow little gorge into Ruin Spring Canyon. The general and others waited there under cover to stop any one who might disturb the Indians while they made camp in Cottonwood. The posse made no attempt to follow, and in the early evening the ambuscade moved on to join the camp.

They had started now towards The Big Trail, and every mile in that direction should give them added security till they reached a point where no one would dare to follow, a point beyond which no pursuer had ever survived. But what about their people held under guard—their gallant braves kept shamefully as prisoners in Blanding? General Posey had promised to accomplish their rescue that night; he knew they would expect it of him; and he cudgled his brain for a way to do it.

He told his people to start before the dawn, and to wait for him in the Butler. Then he rode off in the night on his black mare, sworn to do the impossible. Somewhere on the trail of his people that afternoon, the posse would be dozing on their saddles awaiting the morning. Posey would not hazard finding them, but he would follow the Cottonwood to the old road.

He expected to find his prisoner-tribesmen guarded at some open camp in the streets of the town, their guards in plain view and at the mercy of whoever might plot against them from the darkness. Instead, when he rode quietly into the sleeping town he saw but one light, and it was in the school house. His people were confined in the basement rooms with armed guards stationed at every entrance and perhaps waiting in the rooms above to meet every emergency.

(To be Continued)

THE FLAMING TORCH

There is not a day passes in which this flaming torch of carelessness does not add to its already enormous total of fire destruction.

If fire descended on you tonight, and tomorrow you found yourself without a home, where would the money come from to replace and rebuild what you have lost?

For more than fifty years the UTAH HOME FIRE has stood the test of time, fires, panics and depressions. It has paid millions of dollars in losses, and yet its proudest asset is its reputation for commercial honor and good faith.

FORTY YEARS OF SERVICE

(Continued from page 681)

And of this experience the President's daughter, Lucy G. Cannon,
has written:

The Improvement Era was almost born
in our home—it was at least nurtured
there after its birth. Father sent personal
letters by the thousands. We had several
typewriters and several of us children
learned to typewrite getting out Era letters.
We had a large dining room and an especially large dining room table. This
table would be pulled out and half a dozen
leaves put in it. Then we would all sit
around and some would fold; others would
write. Father was usually seated at the
end signing his name. We had half a
dozen enclosures to put into the envelopes,
so it took us all to get these letters ready
for the mail. Maybe that is the reason I
am so interested in and proud of *The Improvement Era,* because I feel I had a hand
in starting it.   Father's interest in this
magazine has never waned from that day
to this and I think his work for it has
been one of his outstanding contributions
to the Church.

I N THESE brief accounts one can
read of the humble beginning of
the magazine which in forty years
has grown in importance and power
because of the constant message it
has borne, and because of the men
who have fortified it. During all of
these forty years its two senior editors have been either members of
the First Presidency or Presidents
of the Church, successively.

In 1907, the magazine became the
official organ of the Seventies; in
1909, of all the Priesthood; in 1911
of all of the Church schools; in 1924,
of the Music Committee of the
Church; in 1929, of the Young
Women's Mutual Improvement Association.

It was unique for a group of men
and women to go out among the
people without even a sample of
their proposed magazine and seek
subscriptions for it in sufficient numbers to pay for its publication.   A
printed prospectus and the promise
of a magazine to follow was all they
had.   Nothing but the missionary
spirit which characterized that undertaking and which still character-
izes *Era* service, could have brought
success.

Joseph F. Smith, then Second
Counselor in the First Presidency,
and Elder B. H. Roberts, then a
member of the First Council of Seventy, were named as editors of the
magazine which, at that time, did
not exist, and Elder Heber J. Grant,
then a member of the Council of the
Twelve, and a member of the General Superintendency of the Y. M.
M. I. A., was named as manager
with Thomas Hull as his assistant.

The personnel of the magazine
changed but slightly during the succeeding years. Edward H. Anderson, a member of the committee
which President Roberts named,
was made an assistant editor during
the second year of the magazine's
existence, when President Roberts
was released to go to Washington,
leaving Joseph F. Smith and Edward H. Anderson as editors.

Other editors and assistant editors of the magazine have been President Heber J. Grant, assisted by
Edward H. Anderson until the lat-
ter's death, when, in 1928, Hugh
J. Cannon was made editor.   After
the merging of the *Era* and the
Young Woman's Journal, Elsie Talmage Brandley, editor of the magazine for the Young Women, was
made associate editor of *The Improvement Era.* After the death of
Hugh J. Cannon in November of
1930, the writer was made managing editor, and Mrs. Brandley
continued as associate editor.   In
May of 1935, under the direction
of the First Presidency, Dr. John
A. Widtsoe, a member of the Council of the Twelve, was made editor,
associated with President Grant
and Harrison R. Merrill. Once again
death struck, this time at Associate
Editor, Mrs. Brandley, who passed
away August 2, 1935, to be suc-
ceeded by Marba Cannon Josephson.   In January, 1936, the writer
was released to return to his school
work at Brigham Young University,
and Elder Richard L. Evans, the
present managing editor, who had
several years before been associated
with Dr. James E. Talmage and Dr.
Widtsoe in the editorship of the
Millennial Star, in Europe, was
made managing editor, with Mrs.
Marba C. Josephson, associate editor.

During his management of the
magazine, President Grant was assisted by Thomas Hull, later, by
Alpha J. Higgs, and still later by
Moroni Snow.   When President
Grant became editor, the vacancy
he left in the management was filled
by Elder Melvin J. Ballard, a member of the Council of the Twelve,
and at that time a member of
the superintendency of the Y. M.
M. I. A.

In 1929 the General Superintend-
ency of the Young Men's Mutual
Improvement Association determin-
(Continued on page 722)

Watch for the "Era's" New Continued Story.

Above is pictured part of the 52 wagonloads of imported equipment for America's first beet sugar factory, brought into Utah in 1852 when freight from the Missouri River was $500.00 a ton.

For the Well-being of All the People

The establishment and development of the beet sugar industry in Utah represents, in a singular sense, a practical application of one of the fundamental tenets of the Mormon Church—the principle of "temporal salvation."

First ventured in 1852 by early Church leaders, the intermountain beet sugar industry has helped to bring to this people a higher degree of self-reliance and prosperity, which has been a boon both to producers and consumers. It has assured to the housewife a dependable supply of this essential food at a reasonable price; it has provided to thousands of farmers a sure cash crop; and it has increased industrial payrolls. In short, it has promoted the general prosperity and well-being of all the people.

THE AMALGAMATED SUGAR COMPANY is proud of the part it has played in this program. With a genuine feeling of kinship, we, therefore, congratulate the Church leaders on the part they have played in the encouragement of the beet sugar industry; and we congratulate **The Improvement Era**, on the celebration of its 40th anniversary in business.

THE AMALGAMATED SUGAR COMPANY
Ogden, Utah

OFFICERS

M. S. ECCLES, PRESIDENT
H. A. BENNING, VICE-PRESIDENT AND GENERAL MGR,
G. B. RODMAN, VICE-PRESIDENT—SALES
J. R. BACHMAN, SECRETARY AND TREASURER

DIRECTORS

S. F. BALLIF, JR.
G. L. BECKER
E. G. BENNETT
H. A. BENNING
EDWARD L. BURTON

SYLVESTER Q. CANNON
M. S. ECCLES
S. S. ECCLES
STEPHEN L. RICHARDS, CHAIRMAN
J. F. SCOWCROFT
ARTHUR WINTER

Forty Years of Service
(Continued from page 720)

ed that *The Improvement Era* should be increased in effectiveness and distributed more generally over the Church. George Q. Morris, who had been a member of the committee on finance and publications for several years, was made chairman, and two new members, John D. Giles and Stringam A. Stevens, both men of wide experience in such matters, were called to the board and made members of the *Era* committee.

This committee, with Hugh J. Cannon, Associate Editor, and O. B. Peterson as secretary, held meetings at 8 o'clock each morning five days a week for many weeks. A survey covering every phase of the problem was conducted. The results with recommendations contained in a 10,000 word written and illustrated report was presented to the General Superintendency — Elders George Albert Smith, Richard R. Lyman, and Melvin J. Ballard—and with their enthusiastic approval submitted to the Y. M. M. I. A. general board, where unanimous approval also was given.

The report recommended enlargement of the size, scope, and increase of circulation along lines followed by standard national magazines with definite recommendations covering editorial policy, definite fields for feature articles, advertising, circulation and organization.

At this point it was considered advisable to invite the Young Women's Mutual Improvement Association to merge their magazine, *The Young Woman's Journal*, with the *Era*, making one big, representative magazine for the M. I. A. conjointly and the Priesthood, Church Department of Education, Church Music Committee, and other Church agencies. This invitation was accepted and a joint committee representing both boards was formed to lay plans for the combined magazine.

The new committee quickly completed its plans which received the hearty approval and endorsement of the First Presidency and at June Conference of 1929 the joint publication was announced and a Church-wide subscription campaign launched. When the campaign reached its climax more than 44,000 subscriptions had been received— the largest circulation of any magazine in the history of the Church. The newly combined Church-wide magazine was welcomed into the
(Concluded on page 724)

Greetings From Utah's Largest and Finest Hotel

40 YEARS SOON FLY—

WE SINCERELY HOPE TO MAKE TIME SPENT AT THE UTAH, PASS PLEASANTLY . . .

The Utah was Formally Opened June 8th, 1911
2 Years Under Construction

This year marks a milestone in the life of President Heber J. Grant. 40 years ago he founded the Improvement Era—an institution that has been a power for good in disseminating information about Latter-day Saint activities. We heartily congratulate President Grant and the Improvement Era on a good job, well done.

Since 1911, the Hotel Utah has been the leading hotel in the intermountain country. Our modernization program, started in March, 1935, solidly cements the Utah's position as "A Great Hotel in a Great City."

Make the Utah your headquarters when in Salt Lake City—nothing has or will be spared to make your visit most enjoyable.

NOW—Public Rooms are completely air conditioned.

FORTY YEARS OF SERVICE

(*Concluded from page 722*)

field in November, 1929, with an editorial greeting by the First Presidency of the Church.

In 1929, when the two magazines merged, Miss Clarissa A. Beesley, a member of the presidency of the General Board of the Young Women's Mutual Improvement Association, was made associate manager of the *Era*, representing the young women, and in 1930, O. B. Peterson, who had served a number of years with Edward H. Anderson, was named assistant business manager, and in 1933 business manager, at which time Elder Melvin J. Ballard became General Manager, which was a newly created title so far as the *Era* is concerned.

Upon the reorganization of· the General Board of the Young Men's Mutual Improvement Association in 1935, the present officers of the magazine were installed, O. B. Peterson resigning to enter the printing business for himself in California. And so the staff as at present constituted includes the following: Editors, Heber J. Grant and John A. Widtsoe; Managing Editor, Richard L. Evans; Associate Editor, Marba C. Josephson; General Manager, George Q. Morris; Associate Manager, Clarissa A. Beesley; Business Manager, John K. Orton.

The active business and editorial responsibility of the magazine is chargeable to the managing editor.

WITH the passing years, enthusiasm for *The Improvement Era* has grown. From an infant without financial backing except in the faith and love of the young men of the Church, it has grown to be an influential periodical with a circulation of approximately forty thousand, placing it among the well-supported magazines of the nation. It is a member of the Audit Bureau of Circulations, maintains advertising representatives in the principal business markets of the nation, and is a constant visitor in scores of the country's leading libraries.

From the beginning, the magazine has fostered the arts. Young writers of the Church and many from outside have found its pages friendly and have received encouragement by having the best of their material published. Artists as well as writers of all kinds have been

in a place where it will be preserved permanently.

With the Church expanding on every side, with regular stakes of Zion being set up in far distant places and on the islands of the sea, with Church membership and Church branches in many countries, the mission of the *Era* has grown in importance. It is the tie that binds. It is the chain which links stake to stake, ward to ward, branch to branch, mission to mission, and Saint to Saint. Some day, perhaps, it will be important in making for the understanding that must come between nations.

With forty years of splendid history and tradition behind it, built upon faith in the young people of the Church, a faith that is glowing more brightly as the years are passing, and as understanding and knowledge increase, *The Improvement Era* is ready to go forward. Representing the Church, carrying in its pages the most important pronouncements of the First Presidency and General Authorities of the Church, it is a magazine that should be in every home where Latter-day Saints dwell.

The spirit of the *Era* has not changed. For forty years it has been a steady voice in a changing world, a world filled with doubt, with apprehension, with disaster and despair. Those blessed people who have made the magazine a constant visitor to their homes and a constant companion of their children will agree with President Grant when as manager he wrote to the assistant editor, Edward H. Anderson:

Personally, I would not be without the valuable instructions in the *Era* for ten times the price of the subscription. Many complain that they can get a larger eastern paper for less, but this only shows that they do not know how to estimate value. Life Eternal is the Pearl of Great Price we are after, and little, if anything, to aid us in securing it is to be found in the eastern magazines, if they do print more matter; but much is printed that will cause us to lose this, the greatest of all God's gifts to man.

As the radio beam directs the pilot of the air through storm and fog and darkness safely to his landing field, may *The Improvement Era* continue to direct those who read it and heed the messages contained therein into a peaceful, happy, and

FORTY YEARS OF CHANGE

THE TELEPHONE OF THE PRESENT. (SEE PAGE 708 FOR ITS ANTIQUATED PREDECESSOR.)

(Concluded from page 675)

cause they were earnest and sincere and driven by vicissitude they left out every non-essential. Thus was achieved a purity of style that has never been surpassed. It was only when the later crop of American millionaires sprang up that this beautiful simplicity was forsaken for an ugly ornateness that is characteristic of later building. And just as we should return to the colonial period for standards of good taste in architecture, so we can profitably turn to it for instruction in other lines. For the pioneer periods of all history are periods of inspiration. Then it is that stern necessity drives people to do the important thing, and no one has time for traditional nonsense. Just so, the Lord led the Hebrews through the desert for forty years to purge from them the diseased culture of Egypt. Only then were they ready to start a new civilization in the promised land.

X.

TURNING now to our own people, it may be said that with the celebration of the Jubilee Year, 1897, the pioneer phase of Mormonism had ended. Communities had been founded, irrigation had become workable, and economic security had been more or less achieved for the Saints in the mountainous deserts of the West.

Political security, too, for the first time in the stormy history of the Church, was apparently within the grasp of the freedom-loving Saints. With the issuance of the manifesto releasing the Church from the heavy responsibilities of plural marriage, the strategic advantage of foes who sought to wrest political control in the intermountain country was at an end. Statehood had finally been vouchsafed Utah, the spectres of disfranchisement and escheat had dropped below our horizon, and a native son, the choice of the people, was seated in the gubernatorial chair in Utah.

Thus a new era of relative toleration and recognition was opening up before the Saints. Since 1830 they had been ringed about most of the time with intolerant foes. Now after nearly seventy years there came at last the promise of release from the cumulative emotional stress occasioned by constant threat of deprivation of life, freedom, or property.

Some part at least of this grateful change in the situation of the Latter-day Saints is due, I think, to a change in American manners. Who can read biography of the nineteenth century without getting a picture of the typical Yankee of that period as a well-meaning but inflammable creature whose instinct in case of dispute was to resort, not to law, but to the weapons of anarchy? It was an exuberant age, of intemperate speech and mob action, and Mormons were not the only victims of it. Something of this still persists in the feuds and lynchings of some sections of the South and in the disorderly handling of strikes in the North. But in the main, Americans have become more civilized—have acquired more of the virtues of tolerance and submission to the slowness and orderliness of law.

But we are living in topsy-turvy times. Knowledge has seemingly been poured out on the world faster than humanity can assimilate it. We use our wonderful inventions like children playing with new toys... Spurts of progress are made along certain lines, but the result is an unbalanced development... We starve because we have too much... Our moral fibre softens, and, like Esau, we trade our wonderful heritage of colonial and pioneer puritanism for the exciting pottage of the Gentiles.

Our great need is balance—spiritual growth must not be outstripped by material progress. But real spiritual growth does not come by prayer and contemplation alone. It comes by giving and building. The best thing Mormons can do now is the very thing that made the pioneers glorious: forget self in the grand project of "building up the Kingdom." That involves the founding and preserving of self-sustaining communities in which each individual is as interested in the welfare of the others as he is in his own—the building of a Zion of such beauty and loveliness and neighborliness that Christ Himself will want to come and live in it.

UTAH POULTRY PRODUCERS...

"Go to Town"....Through Co-operation

Fifteen years ago a small group of Utah men got together for the purpose of organizing an egg and poultry "co-operative". This was in August, 1922, in Gunnison, Utah. Six months later this local association became a state-wide association, representing more than 50% of all the commercial producers of eggs and poultry in Utah.

The growth of the Association and the corresponding growth of Utah's poultry industry from then on reads like a fairy tale. Tradition has it that the total net export of all poultry products from Utah in 1922, was 10 carloads. Since then, due largely to the influence of the Association on production and export sales, nearly 2000 cars of poultry products have been exported from the state in a single year, with a return to the grower of upwards of $14,000,000 from eggs alone, in a peak year, for one of Utah's largest cash agricultural crops.

EAT MORE EGGS
The Perfect Food

Association eggs are sold in the blue and white carton under the "**Milk White**" trade mark, through leading grocers. "**Milk White**" eggs "top" the market in quality wherever sold. They are "candled" and graded for uniform quality and size. Eat more "**Milk White**" Eggs—for health and economy. They are the perfect food.

UTAH POULTRY PRODUCERS
CO-OPERATIVE ASSOCIATION

ON THE RADIO **K S L**	"MILK WHITE" Morning Matinee with Judith Adams and her Food Talks— Tues., Thurs., Sat. 9:45—Mountain Time

LET'S SAY IT CORRECTLY

BADEN-POWELL. The only way we can be sure we are correct in pronouncing English names is to look for the proper pronunciation and then cling to it. *Ba*—*a* as in *ate*; *den*—*e* as in *silent*; *po* (the *w* you will see is omitted entirely) —the *o* as in *old*; *ell*—the *e* again as in *silent*. The accent follows the *ba* (long *a*, remember!) and *po* (also a long *o!*)

Spectator—preferably the accent follows the second syllable. *Spec*—the *e* as in *end*; *ta*—*a* as in *ate*—and the accent follows this syllable; *tor*—the *o* loses its identity and is pronounced as the *e* in *maker*.

Finale: Since we are now considering the opera, let's get the pronunciation of this word right. *Fi*—the *i* becomes as the first *e* in *event*; *na*—the *a* is pronounced as in the word *arm*; *le*, preferably the *e* becomes as the *a* in the word *chaotic*; a second choice permits it the sound of the first *e* in *event*. The accent follows *na*.

"ENCLOSED article appeared in the *Southwest News Press*, a semi-weekly community paper of this city, under date of April 26, 1937.

"Yours respectfully,
(Signed) "G. W. Wurzbach,"
Member Wilshire Ward.

Enclosed clipping: YOUTH EXONERATED—*By Dan O'Connell*

"Older folks are ever talking about the younger generation. Flaming youth! Begging to differ, we offer an indisputable fact to the contrary. We went to a dance at a Latter-day Saint Church last Tuesday. They have a gathering every Tuesday. Inside was a cross section of high school lads and lassies. Many we recognized and knew that they, like us, were not members of this Church. The evening was one of gaiety and laughter. At the conclusion one of the men got up to say a prayer aloud. All heads were bowed. Quietly, we raised our eyes and glanced about for signs of snickering and flippancy during this solemn moment. All heads were reverently bent. Not a sound was heard. Greatly impressed, we left that fine church. As long as such manifestations of piety are present, youth has nothing to fear."—*Southwest News Press.*

State College, Pennsylvania.

". . . As a boy I helped to get *Era* subscriptions when it was in the volumes about 3 to 10. The M. I. A. was my favorite organization. After these many years I find that the M. I. A. has given me training that I could get in no other organization on earth. It has molded my life and has given me an ideal to do something in this world. I hope the young people in the Church fully appreciate what they have in the M. I. A. organization. I would sacrifice much to be back where I could attend Mutual Improvement Association and give my boy the same opportunity.

"Best wishes and best of luck,
(Signed) "George L. Zundel."

Swiss-German Mission
Leimenstrasse 49, Basel, Switzerland

"WE ASSURE you that the *Era* is one of the finest sources of material for the missionaries that we have. Many have been further distributed among our friends.

"Accept our kindest thanks in advance for the above favor as well as our best wishes for your success.

"Sincerely your brethren,
"Swiss-German Mission,
(Signed) "Sanford M. Bingham, Sec."

Darmstadt, Germany.

"WE, THE missionaries of the Frankforter district of the Swiss-German Mission, also wish to express our appreciation of the *Era* and what it means to us. We can hardly wait each month until it comes, and when it does everything is laid aside until it is read. We really learn to appreciate it when we get so far away from Zion. I read it from cover to cover and enjoy every bit of it.

"Sincerely your brother,
(Signed) "Clark J. Gubler,
"Advisory Elder."

SILENCE WITH A KICK

"EVERY time my wife hears a noise at night she thinks it's burglars and wakes me up."

"But burglars don't make any noise."

"So I told her. So now she wakes me up when she doesn't hear anything!"—*Bystander (London).*

"I UNDERSTAND the Blanks are strict vegetarians."

"Strict! I should say they are. Why, they won't even let their children eat animal crackers."—*Onward.*

DISCOVERY

"SILK stockings were invented in Queen Elizabeth's time," said the man who knows everything.

"Yes," commented another, "but they weren't discovered till the twentieth century."—*Midwest Review.*

ALL THE triple-threat men aren't football players. We know a fellow who can't attend a party without wanting to recite poetry, play a saxophone, or give imitations of Harry Lauder.
—*Judge.*

IT SEEMS a shame that future generations can't be here now to see for themselves all the splendid things we're doing with their money.—*N. S. in the Saturday Evening Post.*

THE SAME ABSENT-MINDED PROFESSOR

PROFESSOR: "I forgot my umbrella this morning."

His Wife: "How did you remember that you had forgotten it?"

Prof.: "Well, I missed it when I raised my hand to close it after the rain stopped."—*Y. C. Messenger.*

Horse sense is stable thinking—*The Safe Worker.*

THEY MUSTN'T BE MISLED

TEACHER: "Robert, if you are always very kind and polite to all your playmates, what will they think of you?"

Robert: "Some of 'em will think they can lick me!"—*Vision.*

MORE RARE THAN HONESTY

DIOGENES was wandering aimlessly around the town with his lantern.

"Still looking for an honest man?" sarcastically inquired a cop.

"No," he snapped, "for a parking place."—*Selected.*

'Tis said—

—This augurs well for **The Improvement Era,** passing the fortieth milestone on a career of increasing usefulness.

—Truth of this modern maxim is proved by your home railroad, more helpful than ever in development of Utah and Colorado after 68 years of faithful transportation service to the Intermountain West.

The Denver & Rio Grande Western was an advertiser in the first volume of **The Improvement Era,** forty years ago, and this railroad's service has contributed to the growth of the great Inland West each succeeding year.

WILSON McCARTHY
HENRY SWAN
Trustees

For transportation information
O. J. GRIMES, Assistant Traffic Manager
24 South Main Street   Salt Lake City

ROYAL GORGE
MOFFAT TUNNEL

SCENIC LINE OF THE WORLD

DENVER & RIO GRANDE
WESTERN RAILROAD

RESERVE STRENGTH

Life, like football, is a game of skill, endurance, and team-work. And, in life, as in football, reserve strength often means the difference between defeat and victory.

Let's think of your family as a football team. You, the father, are the captain and quarterback. You are carrying the ball now, and you're making gains. It looks as if your team will win. But suppose the Head Coach sees fit to take you out of the game. Without your help the remainder of the team—your wife and family—will be disastrously handicapped.

You can provide a "reserve player" to step into your place and help your family win. This reserve player is life insurance; and though it may not be the versatile "triple-threat" man that you are, life insurance is thoroughly dependable and always comes through in a pinch.

Begin now a systematic insurance plan in this strong company. Beneficial agents are willing and competent to help you plan a life insurance program. If you do not know who your nearest Beneficial agent is, write the home office.

BENEFICIAL LIFE
INSURANCE COMPANY

HOME OFFICE—BENEFICIAL LIFE BUILDING, SALT LAKE CITY, UTAH

HEBER J. GRANT, PRESIDENT

Lightning Source UK Ltd.
Milton Keynes UK
UKHW020751251118
332796UK00002B/31/P